T0170583

Under Three
EMPIRES

Under Three
EMPIRES

THE THORNS AND ROSES OF A LIFE

IZYASLAV DARAKHOVSKIY

Bartleby Press
Washington • Baltimore

Printed in the United States of America

Bartleby Press
9045 Maier Road
Suite D
Laurel, MD 20723
1-800-953-9929
www.BartlebythePublisher.com

ISBN 978-0-910155-65-6

Library of Congress Control Number: 2006925733

In memory of my father, an ordinary, hardworking and modest man. He never complained, but did what he had to do in times of both war and peace.

It is my profound wish that society will someday revere the lives and deeds of common people like my father as much as it values and respects the most gifted and talented among us.

CONTENTS

PREFACE

According to my father, my grandfather was fond of the parable about the two envelopes or, as he called it, "The Last Will and Testament." This was a part of our family's lore. The envelopes dealt not with the material side of inheritance but with sage advice and life experiences imparted by the elder generation to the future ones. This story is a reminder of the fortunate and unfortunate times of life.

Grandfather told my father to read the first envelope only at the hardest, most hopeless moments of life when he felt he could not cope with the woes that had befallen him.

During his life my father faced many hopeless situations. But only in 1941, while hiding in the cellar of an abandoned house with a fellow soldier in a village captured by the Germans, did he remember the first envelope. Only ten or twelve feet (four meters) separated them from the Germans, who were celebrating yet another victory. These two men feared that their lives were about to end. They were disoriented and exhausted by the trials and constant defeats of war. At that moment my father thought he heard Grandfather's voice. "My son! You are confused, your soul is crushed, and you have lost all hope.

It is hard for you, impossibly hard, this is the darkest time in your life. But be strong, my son. Pull yourself together. You will have many happy times in your life. Be strong and keep fighting for your life. You will win, you will certainly win." And my father survived.

Many years later, in 1986, during one of the happiest days of my life, my father started a conversation about the second envelope. It was a special time for me. One could even say it was the peak of my professional, academic, and social recognition. It was one of the major events of my life. In a beautiful, official auditorium in Moscow in celebratory surroundings, a group of scientists from all over the large country were awarded the highest scientific degrees: the Doctor of Sciences and Professor of Science.

Presiding over the ceremony was a national leader in the sciences, a vice president of the Academy of Sciences, USSR. In congratulating us, he amazed everyone with his beautiful, intelligent speech. Sitting with a distinguished assembly of scholars, I was so overcome with emotion that I only half listened to his address. Several other thoughts were going through my mind.

Only a few Jewish representatives of managed to overcome the almost insurmountable social, national, religious, personal, and professional barriers to arrive at today's occasion. Scenes from my life and the life of my large family passed before me. Yet I will remember two moments of his speech forever.

First, the scholar said, "You will never again in your life be in such intelligent company as today." And I have often remembered his words. On that day we, 300 newly minted advanced Doctors of Sciences represented nearly 100 different disciplines – Mathematics, Physics, Chemistry, Economics,

Philosophy, Philology, History, Geology, Geography, and so on. I knew his words were true, that I would never again be among such an accomplished group of intellectuals.

His second comment was that new and special opportunities would be opening for us. While more for some and less for others, he continued, "Now your social status is high. You now belong to the elite of society. Materially, your labor will be rewarded higher than in any other field of work." That day in Moscow was special for me.

Back home in the Ukraine while discussing with my father the significant changes in my life, he remembered my grandfather and the story about the two envelopes. Suddenly my father said in my grandfather's voice, "My dear son! Today you are at the peak of success. You achieved something that probably you could not even imagine when you were young. You are a winner. Rejoice. You earned this. But do not forget that in life there are good and bad times. Today is the day to think about what awaits you in the future."

I was standing next to my father in complete confusion. So unexpected and strange it was—and with such odd timing—to hear my grandfather's message from long-ago in these words of warning from my father. At that instant the rosy predictions of a famous academic and the cautionary words of my grandfather swirled together in my head. Paradoxical as it was, the winner of this "debate" would be my grandfather.

It is said that cats have nine lives. I have had only three lives, each under a different Empire. But, as the reader will see, three were enough! The three were different in their goals, emotional intensity, professional activity, usefulness to society, and social status. They were totally different for me and my surroundings as well as in the valuation of me by others and society.

This is a personal story, but through the life of one family the reader will discover a new world of relations between people completely different from the American way of life.

You, the reader, I hope, will be drawn into the drama of my life. You will find a story of a man with a unique ensemble of experiences and how these experiences helped a person not to collapse morally but instead preserve a healthy outlook despite numerous trials and tribulations. I hope you will be able to rejoice with a person who in desperate situations usually came out the winner.

ACKNOWLEDGEMENTS

I t is a great pleasure for me to note with appreciation those who have assisted me during the writing of this book.

Many people have motivated me to write my story. They included some listeners at lectures I have given and even the officer of the Department of Naturalization when I was tested before becoming a citizen of the United States.

In particular, I would like to express my gratitude to two people who over the years have encouraged me. They are Robert J. Trace, former Deputy Attorney General of Pennsylvania and his wife Peggy, my long-time friends. Our frequent meetings and discussions were invaluable

Many thanks to two highly educated and intellectual people who have often been there to assist me. Kenneth Dean has shown a great interest in the manuscript and supported me in many ways. His critical point of view and advice were of great significance. I am grateful to Dr. Kenneth Cauthen, who put a lot of time and talent in helping me edit the book.

There are also two young people, who deserve an extra thank you for making the publication of this book possible. They are Antony Forgione and my son Henry.

Mike Foy has been my good and devoted friend who,

in my first years in the United States, was my guide in my new life and country. It is hard for me to think of this book without Mike's support. He was the first reader, the first editor, the first literary critic and the first reviewer of this book.

And finally, I would like to add a special word of appreciation to the editor Jeremy Kay of Bartleby Press for his wonderful assistance in getting this book ready for publication.

Chapter 1

A Life Worth Less Than a Penny

In 1941 I was five years old. That year was a turning point in the lives of hundreds of millions of people. The Germans invaded Ukraine in July. Soon Yampol, my hometown, in the Southwest Ukraine, was under threat of occupation.

When the Nazi assault began, we did not know how to respond. We were living in a small town far removed from the world at large. Education was not a priority. People never moved from one city to another, not even to those only fifteen or twenty miles away. Most people in Yampol had very little money. They had no understanding of the serious threat the Germans posed. The elders in our town who survived World War I remembered that the Germans were better to the Jews than most Ukrainian and Russian armies. They told us the Germans were civilized and would never kill innocent Jewish people. This misplaced trust would lead to the loss of many lives.

When we first became aware of the Nazi threat, we did nothing. We had no advice on how to respond, nor did we have resources to flee. Some doctors, lawyers, and teachers who had money, were able to evacuate. Others, who worked for the Soviet-run factories, were able to move to the Eastern part of the Soviet Union where there were factories involved

Two years old.

in the war effort. The government needed their skills to produce military goods, so they received assistance to relocate. But we, like hundreds of thousands of other needy people, were forgotten and left to take care of ourselves.

In July my stepmother's father came to visit us from his village, Dzygovka, eight miles away. (My natural mother passed away when I was eight months old.) He told my mother that we had to leave because the Germans were rapidly getting closer.

My grandfather worked on a collective farm and asked the manager for a cart and two horses. He got them because the manager respected him and remembered that he had contributed animals when he joined the co-op. My grandfather collected his four daughters, one daughter-in-law, and five grandchildren, ages one month to five years, including me. He told us that we would leave soon and told us what to bring with us. Two days later grandfather loaded us on the cart, and we headed east, away from the advancing Germans.

On our journey some friends and neighbors from Yampol and Dzygovka joined us. There were five carts in all. My grandfather was not only a strong, hard worker but was also able to choose the best horses. His cart, which I was on, was the guide cart. Our little caravan traveled day and night, and we would make two or three stops at night to sleep. We traveled on pathways bordering the main road, since it was used by the retreating Soviet Army. One night, when the German planes blew up a Soviet army depot, the sky was as bright as day.

We had traveled about four days and had covered about 120 miles when we heard motorized vehicles behind us. Grandfather whipped the horses, causing them to make a sharp turn. We thought the vehicles would be the Soviet Army in retreat. After a couple of minutes we realized with a sinking feeling that the sound hearkened the arrival of German soldiers. Even though I was only five years old, to this day I remember the moment like a bad dream. We all gathered around my grandfather as the German soldiers came closer. At this time my aunt noticed that I was dressed in a shirt that had Soviet Star buttons. Quickly she ripped off the buttons with her teeth. In a moment a strong and menacing enemy stood before us.

The first soldier forced us to raise our arms over our heads. The second soldier beat my aunt in her ribs as she was not able to react immediately due to her partial deafness. The third soldier continuously kicked my grandfather. He had been thrown to the ground while attempting to help my aunt get in line with us. The fourth soldier took another of my aunts behind the bushes, dragging her as he would drag a lamb. The fifth soldier searched our cart but found nothing of value to him. The sixth soldier took our rings, earrings, and watches.

My grandfather was wearing a family heirloom ring. The soldier ordered him to take it off, but he couldn't, so the fascist removed it. The soldier noticed that my grandfather's hands were as hard as rocks, toughened from his fifty years work as a farmer. Suspicious of our activity, the soldier asked him, "Why aren't you taking part in the harvest now?"

My grandfather responded that we were returning from a holiday not far from Kiev. Fortunately, our cart was facing west in the direction of our home. One of my aunts told the soldier, "We are headed home." The Germans told my grandfather to be on his way, so we began our journey again.

After a couple of miles we were still shocked and saddened. The Germans had killed eleven people from the three other carts in our caravan. Most of them were from Dzygovka. I was later told that the victims were young girls. Some of them were raped along with their mothers who were trying to defend them.

From the first moment I saw the Germans, I was gripped with a fear that stayed with me for many years. Every time I hear a motorcycle, I am reminded of the soldiers that confronted us that day long ago.

My grandfather wanted us to go to Dzygovka, but my mother wished to return home to Yampol, which we did. After several days my father returned to us. He was one of the lucky Soviet soldiers not taken prisoner.

Shortly afterward a part of our town became a Jewish ghetto. The ghetto was comprised of two streets fenced in by barbed wire. Our home was outside the fence, so we were not able to live there. My parents, my sister, and I moved into a small room in my uncle's house, where we lived for a year. Every day most of the people in the ghetto were forced to work long hours on the farms and factories, while others built roads. Some people were required to clean the soldiers' quarters and the streets.

One night a tremendous flood swept through Yampol. The deluge of water came upon us so abruptly that no one knew what to do. It was a scene of utter panic and chaos. Fortunately, some Italian soldiers, allies of the Nazis, took doors off the houses and helped save the children in our ghetto. This was the only time we were thankful for what our enemies did.

In September 1942, we found out that our family was to be sent to a German camp. One morning Nazi soldiers came into the ghetto and forced everyone to gather in the street. We were told to take our few belongings, including clothes for winter. People were placed in groups. Some of them were directed to step aside. At first we did not know why we were being separated. Then we were told that our group was going to the local rail station. When the adults heard this, they knew that being sent away on a train usually meant death. This was a terrifying spectacle.

People were wailing and crying, all trying to say goodbye to loved ones, family, friends, and neighbors. In many cases families were torn apart, with parents sent to the train while the children were left behind. In some cases older children were sent to the camp without their families.

Yampol had only one rail line, and we were forced to walk three miles to the station. Some people were unable to make the trip. The younger people tried to help the older ones, but some were shot along the way. There were about 150 of us on the cattle train. No one knew where we were going. The trip took about two days, and the conditions were indescribably bad.

The camp we were sent to was about fifteen miles from Lodigino, in the center of Ukraine. It was located on a small river with Germans on one side and Romanians on the other. We were so "happy" to be controlled by two "masters!"

There were about 350 Jews there. This location had a stone quarry, and we were forced to work as slave laborers. Later we learned that some of the rocks we excavated were used to build a bunker for Hitler near the city Vinnitsa. At times Hitler wanted to be closer to the front lines. No one from Dzygovka was sent to the camp. The elders in our community believed that the eleven Jews who were killed from our caravan were Dzygovka's payment to the Germans. After we were sent to the camp, my mother always questioned why she did not follow her father's advice and go to Dzygovka when we returned home.

Life in the camp was difficult. We lived in barracks built of thin wood. It was not heated, but because there were so many people crammed into each building, we really did not need it. Each barrack was about twenty yards by six yards, and housed from thirty to thirty-five people. Everybody had a little territory, although we were usually packed so tightly that at night we touched each other. There was a barrel with water but no bathroom.

Each day was the same. The men and younger women worked all day extracting rocks, moving them on litters which were loaded onto trucks and then onto railroad cars. Children, starting at seven or eight years old, worked with the older women and handled the smaller rocks. Initially I cared for my younger sister so my mother could work.

Most of our energy was focused just on survival. We had three basic functions to worry about: eating, working, and staying alive.

Sometimes, when new prisoners would arrive, the experienced prisoners would teach the new people how to do the work. The new people would share whatever food they had brought with them. Because our whole focus was on personal survival, we were always struggling for food, a day off and for everything else. Food was always scarce, and our minds were constantly focused on getting more. We were usually given corn with a few noodles boiled in water. Occasionally we received potato skins or rotten potatoes left over from feeding the armies. Twice a week we were given a small piece of bread. When we were given bread or potatoes, it was like a special event.

Although most Ukrainians supported the Germans, some who lived outside the camp, would trade food for our meager possessions. I remember a Ukrainian woman who came into the camp to sell bread and sometimes gave pieces of her loaves to some lucky children. Because my father had training as a furrier and could make hats, he was frequently able to trade with some Ukrainians for potatoes or bread. This was an extra benefit for us. The elderly people and others who could not work were not given a full ration of food, and many died of starvation, including two of my aunts.

We always lived under the shadow of fear and death. There was a major difference in treatment by our German and Romanian "masters." The Germans were interested solely in the work to be done. Those who contributed lived; those who did not were killed. The Romanians routinely verbally abused us and treated us brutally. German soldiers on their day off would take our young women away to be abused. We called these Sundays the "Black Days."

One of my most tragic memories was watching my beloved Grandfather get shot and killed attempting to defend his teenage daughter. This memory still brings tears to my eyes. At other times the soldiers ordered eight to twelve of the oldest men into a small boat. Then they tipped the boat over and watched, laughing, as the older men tried to swim. Some of them did not survive.

We were always worried about being transferred to a death camp. The sick, elderly, and nonproductive laborers, as well as those who were seen as troublemakers, were sent to these camps. Most did not survive. One of the two death camps in Ukraine was Pechora, about thirty miles away from our camp.

For almost 1000 days my family endured the enormous hardship of living in the camp. It was two and a half years of slave labor, physical and mental abuse, and hunger. During this entire period I cannot remember seeing a smile from one Jewish person.

We were finally liberated in March 1944. Some partisans came to our camp and told us that the Soviet army was one day or so away. They also told us to be wary of anyone claiming to be liberators. Sometimes Germans took the uniforms of captured or killed Soviet soldiers and tricked camp prisoners into believing they were going to be rescued only to be killed. The partisans warned us that only when we heard the Russian language being spoken were we to believe their claim.

Most of us who survived suffered severe physical and mental problems. Due to the horrible conditions in the camps, disease was rampant, and broken bodies and minds were common.

The women survivors perhaps suffered the most. They were forced to work the same as the men but also had to care for their children and elderly parents. Many of them were abused and raped by the soldiers.

After the war the government paid little attention to their situation. And most sadly, the consequences for widows continued for a long time after the war was over. With such a limited personal and social life these women were never able to enjoy even simple pleasures until they became grandmothers. These women were the real heroines of the war.

After we were liberated, we returned to Yampol. However, for us the war continued for four more months. Yampol was near the site of a bridge over the River Dnister separating Ukraine from Romania. The Germans bombed it at night and the Soviet soldiers rebuilt it during the day. When we heard the planes approaching we went to the houses in town with deep basements. In my mind I can still see the lights of the planes in the night sky.

In Ukraine, less than 30% of the 2.1 million Jews survived.

Initially, my family was apparently more "fortunate" in that 70% of us survived the prison camp. However, soon we found out that other family members had died in other ghettos. A month later we also learned that four of my father's five brothers were killed as soldiers. In total, my family lost twelve Ukrainian Jewish lives to the Germans.

Our personal struggles and tragedies did not end with our liberation. The propaganda machine functioned so well that there was little sympathy for Jews. Although at first many Ukrainians were kind to us, eventually they were swayed by the propaganda and believed that we were somehow responsible for our plight. Even my father's brother, a decorated war hero, thought we had done something to cause our suffering.

For ten years after the war we were required to state that we had lived in German occupied territory. It was as if we were the people who were guilty. We were marked. It affected the lives and careers of thousands of people. In my case, it delayed my entrance to college for five years and created countless obstacles in my daily life. Many Jews, including members of my own family who had not committed any political or criminal offenses, received very severe punishment without investigation.

For almost 50 years after the war ended we were not allowed to discuss the Holocaust in public. Finally, in December 2005, I, along with other survivors, was given recognition by the Russian government for what we had endured and we were presented with a medal of honor. Then, on January 27, 2006, I was invited by the United Nations to attend the First International Day of Commemoration in memory of the victims of the Holocaust.

I am sorry that so many of the survivors, including my mother, father and many other relatives did not live to be publically acknowledged for their suffering.

More than sixty years later, when one asks, "How can such an overwhelming persecution be kept from happening again?" the words of the German writer, Martin Niemoeller, come to mind:

"When they came for the communists, I was silent, because I was not a communist; When they came for the socialists, I was silent, because I was not a socialist; When they came for the trade unionists, I did not protest, because I was not a trade unionist; When they came for the Jews, I did not protest, because I was not a Jew; When they came for me, there was no one left to protest on my behalf."

Chapter 2

THE BEST WAR

According to some historians, during 5,500 years of civilization, there were about 14,500 large wars. Nobody knows how many local wars occurred during this time, certainly many times more. Following WWII, children in the Soviet Union and other Eastern European countries saw movies, read books, played games, and spoke to each other about the war. It is understandable why this topic became so important to the younger generation. At that time almost every one of us had become acquainted with war early in life. Most had suffered the death of relatives, slave labor, constant dread of death as prisoners of concentration camps or ghettos, starvation, and cold. But the most impressive thing for us, of course, was the heroic spirit of the direct participants in the war. Stories told by them were extremely valuable. Even my father, who never talked much, could not resist my numerous questions and began to share with me his war experiences. Here are three of the unforgettable ones.

First War Experience

By the end of the 1930s Germany and the Soviet Union competed with each other in Europe. Each of them wanted to expand territory, but they stood in each others way. The treaty signed between them on August 23, 1939, allowed them to achieve their goals without confrontation.

On September 1, 1939, Germany attacked Poland. The USSR began to establish a "buffer" zone by capturing part of Poland and Romania and the three Baltic Republics— Lithuania, Latvia, and Estonia. The Government and the Army had been thoroughly prepared for this move. Troops, weapons and equipment, built-up for years, were moved rapidly to these border countries . The Red Army had three or four times as many soldiers and six or seven times more weapons. None of these countries could fight against such huge forces, and they were captured almost without resistance and with minimal fatalities. This so called "march for freedom" noticeably lifted the Soviet Union's confidence regarding success in future ventures in territorial expansion.

Propaganda also played an important role. People in the Soviet Union did not want war, but the Government persuaded the population that it was necessary. They were told it was noble to liberate their neighbors from oppression by capitalists and other exploiters. The State authority used many methods of ideological pressure on those they were going to "liberate."

Years later I had a chance to meet numerous people who had lived in Romania during this time. Some of them became my friends. By profession they were lawyers, doctors, teachers, writers, and workers. One of them was a leader of the underground Communist Party of Romania. For more than twenty years those people of different ages, education, and professions were united in the underground struggle on behalf of the Soviet Union. After Bessarabiay, a part of Romania, joined the Soviet Union in 1940, most of its citizens who were already distrusted, became subjects of oppression or were exiled and imprisoned. Others were forbidden to work in their profession for the rest of their lives. These Romanians told me that they misunderstood the intentions of the Soviet leaders and the reality of life in the USSR.

Sometimes people who were not involved in politics, including children, participated in the propaganda.

When I was five years old my family lived in Ukraine in the town of Yampol. The border of Romania was the river Dnister, about 300 feet wide. We were strictly forbidden by the government to get close to this border, but during spring and summer seasons of 1940, everything changed. The authorities of the town organized festivals, meetings, athletic contests, and concerts on the banks of the river. Children were given candies and cookies. The aim of these events was to show the people on the other bank the advantages of life under socialism—how free and happy was the life of workers, peasants, craftsmen, old people, and children in the Soviet Union. As a five-year old I did not realize that by taking part in such festivals, I was participating in propagandist work. Nor did many others.

At that time my father, along with thousands of other reservists, became a mobilized soldier. After two months of military retraining he was among those who marched into Romania. He was fortunate. At that time Romania as well as Poland, Lithuania, Latvia and Estonia, put up no resistance, and the victory came to the Red Army easily and with minimal casualties.

Second War Experience

The military situation on the Soviet-Finland border was totally different. Negotiations regarding joining parts of

Finnish territory to the Soviet Union began in 1937. After signing the German-Soviet Union treaty in 1939, the demands of the USSR increased.

The USSR tried to annex Finnish land where 20% of the population lived, including towns, villages, and islands that were located near Helsinki, the capital of Finland. The Finnish government rejected this demand, and the war between the largest country in the world was unleashed upon the small country of Finland on November 30, 1939.

The territory of the Soviet Union was approximately fifty-five times larger, and the population was forty times bigger. However, the Soviet Army faced a well-organized and heroic resistance.

The world community tried to help Finland. America and Sweden loaned Finland money, while other countries supplied armament. England and France began an effort to expel the Soviet Union from the League of Nations.

The authority and the prestige of the Soviet Union were severely undermined. Both strategic and tactical actions of the Soviet Army failed. With the support of the world community, the Finns were well prepared for the war. They fought bravely and successfully. While the Soviet Army had six times as many airplanes, nine times more artillery, and one hundred times the number of tanks, the Soviet losses were huge.

According to information issued later, for every Finnish casualty the Soviet Army lost six soldiers. Fortunately, my father was not one of them. But in the end the USSR won the war and got the land they had wanted from the beginning. But the victory, at such cost, was a defeat in morale. Even two such absolutely different leaders, Churchill in England and Khrushchev in the Soviet Union, agreed on this point.

The spirit waned in the Army. The strong statements about the Army's power and Stalin's assertion that if the Soviets had to fight, they would fight but on somebody else's soil were greeted skeptically at home and abroad. The results quickened Hitler's plan to unleash war against the USSR.

In political and moral hindsight this was one of the worst wars in the history of the Soviet Army. The Government and Army's leaders preferred not to speak about this war, but the soldiers could never forget it.

My father compared this war to an exhausting, prolonged run on an unprotected spot that was well kept by the enemy. On the battlefront the Finns pulled off an outstanding defensive military masterpiece. On both sides there were woods and lakes familiar to the Finnish soldiers. Known as the Manegrame defensive line after the name of the Finnish commander in chief, in the minds of my father's generation it was a symbol of an insurmountable impossibility. They used this battlefield to their advantage, capitalizing on any mistakes of the Soviet Army. The soldiers and officers did their best but in vain. For months they could not advance.

The Soviet's battlefield losses were catastrophic. Lone soldiers, battalions, and even regiments, were annihilated. The temperature of forty degrees below zero Centigrade (about 100 degrees below zero Fahrenheit) was a severe test for Russian soldiers. Their uniforms were not suitable for such unbearable conditions. As a result, tens of thousands of soldiers were missing or frostbitten in the Finnish woods and lakes. My father often recalled his comrades-in-arms, including those who had been taken captive. He had no idea how many thousands had been captured or after their liberation how many had been arrested and sent to Stalin's concentration camps. This information only became public during the 1990s.

Third War Experience

Beginning in June 1941, World War II affected every family in the USSR. Before the War, soldiers mostly served their military duty in their native areas. During the first days of the war my father served in a small town named Great Kosnitsa, twelve miles from his home. This town, as well as our home town Yampol, was located on the bank of the river Dnister. It was the Romanian-Soviet border. Since the summer of 1940 when the USSR annexed some Romanian land, it became the Ukraine-Moldova boundary.

The Soviet government did not trust the people of newly joined territories. Therefore the leaders of Red Army issued an order to build a great number of defensive barriers along the coast of the river. They were made of wood, stone, and soil. The army placed machine guns and trench mortars there. They believed the river and these defensive barriers would be a major obstacle for the enemy. In reality not a single shot was fired from these positions. Later some said the cause was treachery of some high military commanders in the Ukraine. I do not know the cause, but I do know what happened to the detachment where my father served.

As soon as German troops appeared on the other side of the Dnister river and began to erect a bridge, the Soviet soldiers saw their commander saddling a horse and riding in the direction of town. Shrinking in the face of danger, the captain left the defensive position and his soldiers by themselves. The soldiers became panic stricken. Soon the experienced solders, including my father, joined the retreat. Everybody took care of himself. Somebody offered my father a seat in a truck, in which there were four soldiers already. In three hours, confident that they had escaped, they made a stop at a small settlement next to a railway station. They needed to decide what to do. Their attempts to get military guidance failed. Suddenly they heard noises of motorized vehicles. "The Germans are coming," someone shouted. All were panic-stricken.

The mighty strength of the enemy, the fear of death or capture by the Nazis was so strong that one would question whether this army could ever be organized again.

An ordinary soldier, poorly educated, poorly informed about the enemy, badly equipped and ill-prepared, and often deserted by his superiors was to meet his invincible enemy face to face alone. He dashed around like an animal, looking like a hunted beast attempting to save his life. He had to bear responsibility for the mistakes of political leaders, war commanders, the KGB, and so on. Now he had to pay the price of his life for all these mistakes.

The five confused soldiers heard noise of the Nazis advancing. After being frozen by fear, they ran away in different directions, some to the forest and others to the cornfield. My father and his companion came upon a small village, where they hid in a basement of a small abandoned house.

Soon German soldiers occupied the neighboring houses, some inside, some outside. They began to shave, to wash, and to talk to each other in loud voices. For two hours these two fearful soldiers were hidden ten feet away from the Germans. With a sinking heart they were waiting to meet their fate. Suddenly everything became quiet. My father and his comrade did not dare to come out of the basement, but they had to do something. They made up their minds to find out what was happening outside.

Everything around was calm. They did not see any Germans. Suddenly they saw an old man near. "Don't be afraid. I saw you hiding here," he said. He told them that the Germans were gathering the people of the village in the square to elect a new local chief and under the fear of death everybody was forced to gather the harvest. The man gave a old pair of trousers and a sport shirt to my father's comrade. He also advised my father to get clothes for himself. They were lucky because it was July, and they did not need heavy garments. The most important warning that he gave was to get a sickle and walk in the road, never hiding. If anybody asked them questions, they were to answer that they were going to gather the harvest.

Thanks to the advice of this smart, kind, and brave man (it was very dangerous at that time to have any contact with Soviet soldiers), three days later my father and his friend came home.

Later my father would say that these two hours in the basement were the most terrible time of his whole life. This in spite of the fact that he survived a prison, a concentration camp, and served in a field-engineering (or combat-engineering) division. His task was to build bridges and other military installations. These soldiers were in the first line of attack usually where there was water or other natural obstacles. They were also the last to retreat. Often under heavy fire, they blew up something they had built only hours before.

My father finished the war in Budapest, Hungary. In October 1945 he was discharged from the army, and he—a soldier—returned home. His youngest brother also returned home, but his four other brothers were killed on the battlefield. Eleven of my mother's relatives also fought at the front of the war. Seven of them were killed. This was the cost my family paid in this horrible, yet successful, war. A heavy price was paid by most families of the Soviet Union. The victory over the Germans cost twenty-seven million lives.

I remember as a child asking my father: "Which war of the three was the easiest?" "From the point of view of a soldier," said he, "the best war is the one that was never begun." I find these simple and wise words of my father deeply insightful. I question why history so vividly remembers the likes of Genghis Kahn, Napoleon, and Hitler, who started major wars, but gives so little recognition to world leaders who worked hard and successfully to prevent the horrors of war from ever occurring.

Chapter 3

WHY WOULD A MOTHER FORGET HER CHILDREN'S BIRTHDAYS?

We emerged from the concentration camp physically exhausted from hard labor, psychologically fractured, and in large measure, with destroyed personalities. For nearly a thousand days we were in the ghetto and the camp. A thousand days of hard, slave labor. A thousand days of living in hunger marked by suffering, horror, hatred, courage and hope. A thousand days without a shred of happiness.

The Romanians were inventive in their choice of torture: daily beatings, debasement, and rape. No mercy was shown to anyone young or old. Many of us became ill with inflammation of the lungs—some of us two or three times— as well as dysentery and typhus. I had dystrophy during the war and long after it was over. It affected my overall health.

Nearly every member of my family received an "inheritance"—lifelong chronic illness. At twenty-eight years of age my mother's back was badly damaged. She had such severe dislocation of her spinal discs from hard labor, that her capabilities were limited the rest of her life. From early childhood, my sister suffered from heart disease. I have severe arthritis. Some members of my family developed psoriasis and diabetes because of what they experienced.

A Mother Who Forgot Her Children's Birthdays?

A day after our liberation from the camp we were being registered. We discovered things that, even to this day, bring a shock when I think of them. The mother of my sister's husband, Udle Ikman, was in such a state that she could not remember her children's birthdays. The officer who was registering us politely asked four or five times for those dates. After a long pause she finally replied that her children's birthdays were the 15th, 16th, and 17th of May. This answer stunned the inspector, and he asked whether any of her kin present could help her with the answer. After a minute he ceased any verification and recorded exactly what the poor woman had said. He realized that what this woman, and thousands of others, had endured in concentration camps and ghettos, could make a loving mother forget her children's birthdays.

This mother was a woman of small, delicate stature. The overseers in the concentration camp began harassing her, often telling her that she was working badly and that she would-be sent to another camp.

The job of mining stone, transporting it, loading it onto trucks and trains does not need slackers.

She was so frightened of being sent to the Pechora death camp that she gathered all her resources and strength that she could find in her fragile body and focused them on her work. This continued for twenty months. It is no wonder that after such lengthy slave labor, serious memory gaps would appear in a thirty-two year-old woman.

Soon she had to endure, another horrible tragedy. Her husband was killed in the war. Still she survived and this woman was able to pull herself up, raise her children well, and help each get a career and a place in life. Her youngest son, Leo, became my brother-in-law and a close and dear friend. He and I both celebrate birthdays in May, I on the 14th and he on the 15th. For him the middle of May is almost a whole week of celebration. From the 14th to the 17th he marks the birthdays of people close to him.

Treatment of Soldiers by the Government

Stalin's treatment of a person imprisoned by the enemy never changed. Tens of thousands of military prisoners of World War II received up to ten years in a gulag on the dictator's orders. Whether he was captured alone or with a whole division, he was punished. No one considered the fact that usually his commander and his superiors all the way to the top of the government were responsible for the surrender.

From 1941 through 1944 I was in Nazi occupied territory. Nobody thought about it then, nor was allowed to. At the beginning of the War I was only five. Neither my mother nor my month-old sister would consciously choose to endure a concentration camp and all the horrors of the Holocaust. It is possible that the government was partially responsible for the fact that hundreds of thousands of people living far from industrial centers and rail stations could not evacuate to the Eastern part of the country.

After the war the government refused to pay meaningful attention to those who were crippled doing their duty, nor to the wives and children of those killed.

Most of the men in my large family were killed in battle, and the rest were casualties of war. I remember that in my childhood I could not find the courage to look in the eyes of a very close and dear relative of mine, Boris.

He came back from the front missing both his arms. He was about thirty then. He could not dress, shave, or fasten his shirt buttons by himself. He was dependent on others for things large and small.

Before the war he was a carpenter. Now he could not dream of such a job. Regretfully, he had no other education, and with the state of his health, there was no chance of getting a new profession. His government paid pension was only about 10% of the minimum that he needed to survive.

One of our acquaintances gave him a position of buyer. In accordance with the existing laws, each farm household was obliged to sell a part of their production to the government at reduced prices. The buyer went to various villages and used all kinds of pressure to secure a purchase of produce. He immediately turned it over to a government warehouse. Boris was not prepared for such a job, which became clear six months later.

The large difference between procurement and market prices opened up the possibility of fraud. People working with him who were experts in the job took advantage of his inexperience and reaped huge profits, while he ended up in prison.

At his sentencing, the government defense attorney asked that consideration be given to the defendant who was a wounded war veteran. He was a victim mainly due to his inexperience. Many could vouch for his previous spotless reputation. The prosecutor and the judge ignored the pleas and sentenced him to the maximum eight years in prison. After he was released, he was not only a physically but also a spiritually broken man.

Something similar happened to my father's youngest brother Alex. He went to the front as a youth at the start of the war and served until a week before Victory Day. Several times he was wounded and shell-shocked. After his last wounds he spent almost a year in a hospital. He returned home without an eye and could not see well out of the other. The elbow of his right arm was not functional, and there were three pieces of shrapnel in his body that bothered him until the end of his life.

Despite this, when he was in trouble with the authorities, no one cared about his war record. No one took into account that he gave his youth and health to his country and that he, like thousands of other eighteen to twenty-one year-old invalids of war with no profession or education, could not without help from the government reenter civilian life in a normal way. During the war these young people quickly proved themselves as soldiers. They knew the value of life and death, and became accustomed to fame and respect for their wartime feats. After the war the value of life quickly changed. Many of them were absolutely unprepared for life in peaceful conditions. This was one of the biggest postwar tragedies! In every city, in every large or small town, many of yesterday's honored soldiers were without education, without a trade, ignored by society, and lived pathetic lives. Many committed suicide.

The government also forgot the wives and children of the war dead. Besides the mostly symbolic pension of the dead father and husband, I cannot remember an instance in which even one of my eight aunts whose husbands died in the war received any help from the government. The same was true of all of my fourteen cousins. They never had a father but were given no assistance in getting a job, an apartment, education or even a stay at a government resort or summer camp for children. Besides that none of them was ever invited to a concert or a Day of Victory celebration for which their husbands and fathers gave their lives.

As soon as those children reached the age of seventeen or eighteen, however, the government quickly remembered them and drafted them into the army. In peacetime my cousins served in the deserts of Central Asia, on the steppes of Kazahstan, on the shores of Barents Sea, and on the ships in the Black Sea fleet. Time passed. Later the grandchildren of those who died in World War II served in the Army. All of us, representatives of three generations, my father's, mine and my son's, did not forget the "trouble" the government bestowed on one member of our family, the WWII soldier.

Hunger

Before I could eat my fill after living in the ghetto and the concentration camps, hunger once again was knocking at the doors of nearly every home.

In 1947 we suffered the beginning of the most horrific period of famine in the history of the country. It began with serious malnourishment followed by acute malnourishment. Finally, there was hardly any food at all. Tens of millions of people suffered from hunger, and thousands died in the cities and villages of Ukraine, Moldova, Volga region, and other regions of the large country.

It is hard to describe what hunger does to the body. Your eyes burn, and the mind is focused solely on some way to get something to eat to ease the pain. No matter how hard you try, no matter what you do, you cannot escape that desire.

A serious situation developed in our family. My father had a full time job but, because of her health, my mother could not work. In addition to our family of four, my father also supported his three younger sisters and a blind aunt. Anything that by some miracle appeared on our table was divided eight ways. Each day there was less and less food. We ate once a day, and soon every other day. The main dish was soup in which, on a lucky day, we could find a cabbage, a potato or a potato skin, or a spoonful of noodles or oatmeal.

Father took all sorts of measures to find a way out of this hard situation but without success. News that a neighbor or a relative died of hunger was received less emotionally than two or three months before. When I became an adult, I tried to imagine how hard it must have been for my parents to witness the suffering of their children. But we were lucky. Help came from three sides.

Alex, my father's youngest brother married a country girl. There was no wedding as such, but a dinner was given for people closest to the couple. No banquet of my future life and no delicacy could even compare to that wonderful dinner. After long months of hunger I could finally eat my fill. I even received two slices of bread for later. It was a great celebration for the stomach, even though for two days afterwards I suffered a tremendous stomach ache since my body was not accustomed to such an excess of food. It didn't matter. I was not hungry! It was only one day, but what a sweet feeling!

My uncle's bride's family had a cow, a kitchen garden, and a farming plot. Their life was easier than that of nearly everybody else. I don't know the details, but in accordance with an agreement, my father's brother took it upon himself to support his aunt and sisters for three months. Now whatever we had on the table was divided four ways instead of eight. The happiness was short lived since soon there was nothing to share. It didn't matter whether the division was by four or eight.

The brother of my natural mother lived in the same town. He worked in a bakery. Seeing the suffering of our family, he offered his help. He promised to give us a loaf of bread every three days; later, when times got better, my father would repay him. This was like manna from heaven.

To this day I can see this long awaited and priceless, heavy, half-raw brick of bread which mother, with great precision, would try to divide to last three days. She would then divide the small pieces among the four of us. This kind act of my uncle saved us from death by hunger.

My stepmother had three sisters and two brothers. All the sisters' husbands died in the war, but the brothers returned home safely. Her oldest brother ended the war in Belorussia, was married there, and worked as a blacksmith at a railroad depot. When mother wrote him a letter, he promised to help.

Everyone in the former USSR knew that Belorussia was the land of potatoes. At any time almost every family had a store of potatoes, especially for the winter. In addition, besides salary, the railroad workers also received modest but crucially important food packets. They also had a variety of other benefits including a yearly round trip to any town in the country. My mother's brother soon came for a visit, bringing with him a bucket of potatoes. We survived!

Citizen of Seven Nations

Father's sister Frieda married in 1948. Her husband Avrum, born in Romania, was a religious scholar. People with that much education in that country at that time were not needed. Being an industrious man, he worked forty-five long years as an unprofessional worker at a hospital in Moldova. Life was complicated, and there was no time for questions and stories, even with a family. All we knew was that in the 1920's and 1930's life scattered his family around the world.

In 1987 I was in Paris at an International Seminar. I met a man named Yacov Sandler. I learned that in his childhood he lived in Romania then left for Israel. In 1929 after one of the mass murders of Jews in Palestine, he was the only survivor of a large family. Soon he found himself in France.

Being a gifted man, especially in languages, he received an education at one of the prestigious Paris universities. Due to a difficult situation in the country, he moved to Poland in search of work and happiness.

In 1939, that part of Poland was absorbed into the USSR, and Mr. Sandler became a citizen of a country new to him. Thousands of people in his situation soon were shipped to Siberia, since the Soviet government regarded them all as an enemy of the people. Mr. Sandler escaped that fate. He was an expert in languages, an excellent translator, he spoke several languages fluently, including Romanian, German, English, French, Polish, Russian, and Ukrainian. Unable to find a job close to his qualifications, he became a bookkeeper at a small paper factory and lived in Lvov, in West Ukraine until June 1941. That summer Nazi and Ukrainian nationalists in the Vuletsky Mountains near Lvov shot a large group of Polish and Jewish intelligentsia. Since Sandler was in an obscure position, he, fortunately, escaped inclusion on that terrible list.

Later, like hundreds of others, he was placed in the Yanovsky concentration camp outside Lvov and experienced all the horrors of camp life—hunger, cold, and fear. By some miracle he survived.

Since at times the Germans used him as a translator, after the war he was denounced, and in 1946 was exiled to Siberia for seven years.

Along with exiles from the Baltic countries, Moldova, Western Ukraine, and Belorussia, he personally found out what taiga (dense forest territory) and bogs were and what it was like to build new settlements in places where no human had ever set foot before. People who knew said that the lives of people forcibly transported to those places were even more horrible than the fate of gulag prisoners. Although material comforts were meager in the camps, they were fed and had a cot in the barracks. In the milieu of the exiles there were instances of cannibalism. Sandler endured these severe tests. His knowledge of several languages helped him to move soon to one of the cities in Siberia. In 1957 after rehabilitation he became a lecturer in a Pedagogical (or teacher's) college.

In 1987 in Paris I shared a hotel with him. He was happy after fifty years to be in Paris again, able to meet some friends of his youth, remember those who could not be there, and answer dozens of questions from his French audience about his life. Later I found out that Yakov was a cousin of my aunt's husband.

After the fall of the USSR fate forced him to change his country of residence again. He moved to Australia, where his sister had lived since 1941, and then on to Germany, where his daughter had a job and citizenship. This is the fate of a man on whom the tumult in Europe, the Middle East, WWII, the Holocaust and Siberia left deep marks. It is a "story about geography" of a man who in his lifetime was forced to change his citizenship six times, but in none of the seven countries did he feel truly happy.

Chapter 4

LIFE IN A SMALL UKRAINIAN TOWN
A Way Of Life In the USSR

My ancestors lived and worked in Yampol for many centuries. I always had the warmest feelings toward this small place with a population of about ten thousand people.

Yampol was a town with amazing beauty, especially during the summer time. I could walk around and see a vast variety of lilacs, acacias, cherry, apple, and plum orchards and vineyards as well as fantastic wheat and grain fields. The curving shores of the Dnister River, the Ukraine's second longest river, the picturesque places along the very tiny Rusanovka River, and other special places have always provided me with precious memories. It is perfectly natural, of course, to have such feelings for one's birthplace, the place where everything happened for the first time.

In Yampol I experienced my first steps, my first words, my first (and I guess) my most devoted friends, my first successes, and first troubles in life. Here I experienced my first feelings and first love without requital, my first serious independent decisions, and my first understanding of the realities and even cruelties of life.

When I was eight months old, I lost my mother. She

died from a blood infection which began at my birth. Medicine was not available and had it been our financial situation did not allow for the costs of medicine or adequate medical help.

"Thanks" to certain neighbors and relatives, sometime around the age of two and a half I was told that I did not have a mother like other children, but merely a stepmother. There is an old Russian tradition that says, "Expect nothing good from a stepmother."

From five to eight years of age I lived in a ghetto and then a fascist camp with my stepmother and little sister, who was only one month old at the time. Life in the ghetto and in concentration camps has been described in many books, movies, memoirs, museum exhibitions and documents. For each of us, however, it was a unique experience.

A year after the war there was great starvation and many other hardships in Ukraine. The question of life or death continued to be part of my experience.

From the end of the war until the mid-1950s, we knew nothing about television. Nor did we have athletic facilities. In fact, there was only one bicycle in the whole town. Most of the time children played outside. We usually played games such as volleyball, basketball, soccer, and chess. We also swam in the river. Although our parents forbade us from swimming without adult supervision, nothing could split us and the river apart. Consequently, tragedies happened to some of our friends. Every year someone drowned or disappeared under the ice in winter. Yet it was through these challenges that we formed our personalities and strong will. We learned to overcome difficulties and the biases of people around us. By winning, we learned to make people treat us with respect. This is quite different from today when parents are hesitant to leave their young children for a matter of minutes, let alone hours on end.

The post-war years were difficult. Our fathers were soldiers of World War II. Many children grew up without their fathers. Their mothers had to play dual roles. Similarly, the children had to assume additional responsibilities. As is always the case some children were attracted by good and others were attracted by something different.

Sports were important to me. Like my friends, I always tried to be the best. More important to me than sports was reading. The library was my second home. I doubt that any of my friends read more books than I did. Not only did I read and analyze books, I was completely entranced, living the lives of the books' heroes. Books gave me knowledge, taught me to dream and to think about the future.

However, the main reason that I loved reading was because the books exposed me to a new and better life. My own life was quite restricted. It was impossible for me even to speak about the travels I dreamed about. Until the age of seventeen I had not been further than twenty-five miles from Yampol with the exception for our attempt to flee at the outbreak of WWII. My travels, short as they were, were only for basketball and volleyball competitions. However, nothing could stop me from dreaming.

I truly believed that I would be able to do something really important in life, and I tried to glorify myself and my town not in the distant future but at that time.

As time passed I realized how unrealistic my dreams were. While these were deeds not accomplished or even attempted, they were ambitions of a boy growing up to be a young man.

In the beginning I wanted to be a teacher and, of course, the best one possible. I read more than before, especially specialized literature. As a result I started to treat critically methods of teaching that were used by some of my teachers. That gave me quite a bit of trouble. I also thought of becoming a doctor. At that time no one could treat conjunctivitis.

When I told the doctor about my red eyes, the sharp pain, the purulent discharge and tears, all of which limited my reading, his solution to my problem was to read less. That was unacceptable to me. I thought a lot about the doctor's response. At that time I felt that I was the one to find the right treatment for this illness. Again I turned to books that continued to fuel new interests. The more books I opened, the broader the world became to me. I even dreamed of cross breeding different animals to develop superior species to surprise the world. I also wrote poems. I dreamed of being a philosopher, a politician, a geologist, or entering some other profession.

My childhood experiences were the same as millions of my peers. We were naive. As children we had not lived long, and we ignored the opinions of adults and their bitter experiences. We believed in words, especially in the words of the press. We did not realize the difference between words and real deeds. Even where we found injustice and lies, we sincerely believed these were exceptions. Our leaders, our government, and the whole social system were presented to us as perfect, and we did not disagree.

Between eleven and twelve years of age my perception changed. I thought differently about the people around me and the town where I lived. Sometimes it seemed that I stopped loving my town. Only affliction, loss, failure, and even the risk of death were associated with it.

I felt the arrogance of people who were just a little better off than others. I knew from experience what poverty was.

The life of rich people was one I could only imagine. Having the example of my parents, I knew the situation of uneducated people. Hence I was impressed by people who were educated, even though I could not imagine the barrier between people of different income, origin, and position in society.

The official policy of the government denied all that, and I believed what they said. How could it be different? In the socialist system we were taught that people are judged by their personal talents, their personal qualities, their attitude to work, and their political activity. People were not judged by wealth or position in society. I had started to understand life more objectively.

I compared life and the system of subordination in my town to a pyramid.

At the base of the town's society were farmers, laborers, and craftsmen—hard working and open- hearted people. There was nothing to fight for between them. A person at the next level even a bookkeeper was arrogant towards a laborer. In turn the bookkeeper was treated in the same way by a teacher or an engineer. The banker treated teachers with indulgence and vice versa. The president of a company was above everybody according to this hierarchy.

At the very top of the pyramid was not the company president but a doctor. Everyone knew his or her place, and nobody and nothing could change this structure. Intelligence, knowledge, appearance, talents, diligence, purposefulness, musical or athletic achievements of a boy or girl—all these qualities were not enough to overcome the hierarchy.

However, the pride and vanity of the so-called "noble" people of the city were put aside when they had to depend upon others who had a higher position or the ability to get what they needed done.

It was sad to see how everyone fawned on the man who headed the trade network in the region. Although he might be nearly illiterate and rude by nature, he had one of the most important positions in town. He allocated goods in short supply. Of course, bribes affected his allocation decisions.

At the beginning it was food and clothing that were in short supply. Later drugs, TV sets, refrigerators, motorcycles, and so on were scarce. For decades the Government was unable to provide the market with the necessary quantity of goods. Everyone depended on the moods and whims of this powerful man. In the end he decided what you would own. He and other people of the trade network in the country knew how to make big money illegally. They got rich. With money, anything could be purchased, even university diplomas and scientific degrees.

However, those involved in illegal activities had a fear of being caught and losing the protection of the communist party boss and their "sweet" position. If caught, some of them could go to prison for a few years.

In contrast, members of the Communist Party Committee and the Soviet Government could have absolutely everything, often free of charge. There was nothing and no one for them to be afraid of. Within a particular region they were like kings. Their word and wish were the law for everyone. Their opinion was final. They had no fear of anyone or anything.

For twenty years (1944-1964) Mr. Ivan Rudenko was the Secretary or the leader of the Yampol district Communist Party Committee. No one can remember even one substantial accomplishment during his leadership. Nevertheless, his name was remembered by people for a long time after he left his position.

He seemed polite, at first, but quickly became known as a

petty tyrant and an extremely cruel person. It seemed that nothing in life gave him more joy than seeing people humiliated and demolished. He was a real artist in taking people down. I remember a teacher who became a drunkard from such treatment. Some families were broken when the women were forced to have a sexual relationship with Rudenko in order to protect their jobs. Other people were laid off from their jobs for no obvious reason. Many lost their income and had to leave their families and relatives, their homes, and their friends and move to a new place.

While it always has been difficult to find a job in a small town, it was even harder to get a job in a big city. To live in a big city, you needed to have a stamp on your passport as a permit to live there. To get that stamp, you had to have a job, but to get the job you had to have that stamp. These requirements were a joke even to a child, but it was the reality. To get out of that vicious circle, one needed to be clever.

Those who knew about Mr. Rudenko's behavior kept silent for a long time. When it became impossible to tolerate this situation any longer, some citizens began to write anonymous letters of complaint to his bosses in Kiev, the capital city of Ukraine. There was no reaction. After awhile, a few people gained the courage to co-sign their letters of complaint and supported their complaints by secretly taking pictures.

The pictures depicted everything that happened during one week at this leader's residence. Included was the house number and a clear view of the residence along with the license plates of cars so there would be no doubt about the subject of the pictures. They showed how Mr. Rudenko daily received a variety of bribes: sugar from the sugar plant, dairy products from the dairy, fruits and vegetables from collective farms, even flowers and mops. Everybody knew that he accepted bribes, but this was the first time such serious, strict, incontestable proof was provided.

During the next three months inspectors who examined this case concluded that Rudenko had done nothing illegal against the citizens of Yampol. Furthermore, the five people who signed their complaints were punished by Rudenko himself. The man who organized the complaint letters was classified as mentally ill.

Due to a reorganization within the political party system, the government reclassified the Yampol region as a part of another area. Rudenko's party position changed, and he was relocated to a bigger city. He became the Chairman of the City Executive Committee, a position second in command and, for him, a lower position in the hierarchy. Rudenko could not tolerate such "an insult". He died from a heart attack. Two sharks could hardly survive in one place.

Clearly the Soviet political system did not operate fairly. Consider the example of a young man who worked as an agriculturist. He was good in his profession. Later he started to work in a regional Communist Party Committee. As a Committee member he had tremendous authority despite the limits of his background. Yet after holding his new political position for one week, he started directing industrial leaders, a music school principal, and a leading doctor.

People used to joke that Party Committee members could even direct ballet. Everyone understood the situation, but nobody argued with the Party. That was a risky business. By complaining, a person could lose his job, be imprisoned, or be repressed in some other manner. Such abnormal conditions led to a different type of human behavior than we know in America. Some people always kept silent, while others who due to their job position had to express their view, always tried to find out the opinion of their boss and to mold their own opinion accordingly. A popular Russian joke used to be: "I do not know what my leader will say at the end of this meeting, but I share his opinion." It was a rule that the Leaders were the last to give a speech during Patty meetings. This mentality was necessary for survival.

I learned this gradually and with difficulty. This was absolutely different from what I had read in books and newspapers. Even in school I realized that nothing is that easy. I found out that teachers treated students based on the social position of their parents. That was the most scary discovery for me. Yet I did not realize that school as an element of the social system was probably similar to the system itself.

To be honest, I started to lose illusions gradually. The school was the last of them. I literally began to stop feeling the ground under my feet. I knew for sure that I could rely only on myself. I did not have the starting point of large family savings or contacts in the government bureaucracy. My basic starting point in life was a great desire and ability to learn and a diligence and persistence in achieving those goals. Yet in reality it did not matter how much I studied, worked, improved my personality, or involved myself in sports and art. Despite my initial efforts to a large extent my future had been limited by my parents' social position. The son of a teacher or a doctor could become a teacher or a doctor, while the son of a farmer or a laborer would continue the trade of his parents.

While I had the highest grades among one hundred school graduates, I did not receive the highest award for scholastic achievement, a special medal. These medals that year were given to three students: a son of a member of the town executive committee, a son of the town's department of education, and a son of the school teacher. They "earned" the medals. With this medal I would have had a chance to get into one of the universities without taking entrance exams. Without it I had to take the required seven entrance exams. I was afraid of oral exams because they provided the examiner with great opportunity to judge subjectively. The loss of this award for me, a graduate-representative of a national minority, meant closed doors at most universities and colleges.

In 1954 I planned to enter the Lvov Technological University, in western Ukraine. Even though I received a

A photograph of
me as a soldier.

higher score than was required for admittance, I was not
accepted as a student. The examiners' committee sent me a
letter explaining that there was an unexpectedly large number
of applicants from Poland. Consequently, they could only
accept some of the students with scores like mine.

Instead I attended a technical college where I graduated
with honors, enabling me to be in the top five percent of the
graduates who would be admitted to the University.

According to the law I did not need any further entrance
exams. I should have become a student automatically. The
University again rejected my application. The authorities said
there was a mistake in the admission papers. I would have to
wait longer to become a student.

I was drafted into the Army, where I tried twice to enter
the Military Institute of Foreign languages. In all it took me
five long years after graduating from the technical college to
become a student at Chisinau State University in Moldova.
These years included three years of military service in the
deserts of the Middle East and the foothills of the Pamir
mountains, and also two years working the virgin soils of
Kazakhstan and as an accountant in the Ukraine. By the time
I entered the University, many of my former, non-Jewish,
classmates had become teachers, engineers, agriculturists, etc.

As time passed, I graduated from the University with
honors. I became a scientist and worked as a Department
Chairman and a professor at the Academy of Science, the most
prestigious scientific research institution in the former USSR.
Over the years the bitterness I felt toward my teachers had
passed. But I never had the desire to return to my high school
and meet those people whose duty was not only to teach
students about honor and justice but to follow these values in
their own lives.

Many of my friends and acquaintances of my nationality followed paths similar to mine. They were also unsuccessful in applying to universities in the Ukraine, especially in such cities as Kiev, Lvov, and Odesa. Striving for a college education and profession, they went to the universities in other republics and regions.

In the beginning, they applied to schools in cities such as Voronezh and Tula, a four to six hour train ride from Moscow. Then they looked further to cities on the Volga River such as Kazan and Samara. Continually facing irresistible obstacles, many of my friends applied to schools in Siberia, in cities such as Yekaterinburg, Chelyabinsk and Novosibirsk. One of my relatives ended up going to a school in Vladivostok, which was about 6,500 miles away from his native town in the Ukraine. He had to go on a train to get there. Planes were not an option at that time. This train ride took three to four weeks one way. Our experience of "exploring Siberia and the Far East of the USSR in order to get a college education and to enter a profession happened to be very helpful for our children twenty five years later.

In the United States I compare my bitter experience of becoming a student in the USSR with the rules for becoming students at universities in the USA. I feel proud of young Americans. Even in a nightmare these young Americans could not imagine the experience of their peers in other countries, even the best of students.

Step by step I was learning about life. My views on many things continued to change, including views of own home town. I started to learn the history of that place that was distant from the noisy expressways of civilization.

In past centuries Mongols, Tartars, Turks, Greeks, Poles, Germans, Romanians and Italians came and left Yampol.

During the October revolution of 1917 and the Civil War of 1918-1922, many armed groups of different political persuasions captured and left this town several times. Each of them made demands for horses, food, and clothing to support their people. There were some that simply wanted to destroy everything they encountered. Poles despised Ukrainians, Germans killed Jews, Ukrainians disliked Russians, and the Russians, as the major nation, ignored the interests of people of other nationalities.

It is not so surprising that after five centuries of confrontation, wars and destruction, the town experienced little progress. It became a cyclical process. People grew their food in difficult conditions, built houses, and tried to improve their living conditions. However, their efforts were continually destroyed. There was always a different conquering army that damaged, burned, robbed and killed. There was no way out. What ever people did, no matter how much they worked, however hard they tried to do their best, the result was always the same – poverty.

Sometimes I visualize my forbears who lived just decades ago and those who lived centuries ago. Because of their nationality and their faith they were humiliated and victimized by others. They tried to move up the social ladder, but as soon as they could earn something for themselves and their families, someone's bad will knocked them back down. They were fortunate just to survive.

Each generation had to start almost from scratch. That was the destiny of my town. That was the destiny of my family.

That was the destiny of millions other people.

During the 1970s and 1980s throughout the soviet union, thousands of books, articles, and brochures were published about the history of cities and towns, villages and settlements. These publications were about a variety of historical events, people, and places. The perceptions of the authors varied widely. Nevertheless, one conclusion could be drawn from all these writings. During the last one hundred and fifty years in Europe social, economic, religious, and national problems increased significantly. By opening its doors to immigrants, the United States not only established the foundations for its future growth but also significantly reduced the level of social, economic, religious, and national problems increased significantly. By opening its doors to immigrants, the United States not only established the foundations for its future growth but also significantly reduced the level of social unrest for Europeans. Without America, the long list of tragic effects in Europe would be much longer.

Chapter 5

COLLEGE EDUCATION:
Five Years Of Climbing The Wall

Finally, I was a student. I liked everything at the University. My dormitory room seemed like a castle compared to the soldiers' barracks. I shared it with four other students.

My student scholarship covered seventy-five percent of my food expenses. The campus had a library, sports facilities, and a theater. The lecture rooms were quite good. The University's main auditorium was solemn and elegant. I was surrounded by young and interesting people.

I appreciated everything—the lectures, seminars, and exams. All these ordinary things, I treated like something special.

I valued and respected many of my professors. Some of them were brilliant. The most important, respected person among the faculty was the Dean of the Department of Economics, Dr. Marlen Makeenko. He earned that respect because he was well-educated, well-mannered, intelligent, and a great lecturer. Because he was also quite young, it is easy to understand why he was popular among the students.

I can remember the first time I met him and heard his first lecture. He addressed each of us freshmen by last names. When there were questions or misunderstandings about the process for arranging students in study groups, he patiently explained the reasons for the particular student's placement. Furthermore, he revealed a caring attitude; he knew personal information about all his students. We joked, "If you want to know more about yourself, ask the Dean."

He seemed to give that first lecture in one breath, without looking at his notes. At that time we knew also about his work as a researcher. He was working towards his second doctorate the highest degree in economics in the USSR. Students admired him and described his place among other teachers as "whale in an aquarium." While teaching us, he shared his perceptions of life. My professor was the ideal teacher in my eyes. I tried to model myself after him in later years.

However, the Dean's qualities that were appreciated by students irritated his colleagues. At the beginning it seemed to me that in such a group of coworkers there should not be any problems. Basically, every teacher had equal opportunity to teach and to do research work. At that time, research in economics required no special laboratories, or equipment, or scarce materials. Nobody knew about computers. The financial factor was not important. The salary of college faculty, as well as those in medical and other fields, did not depend on the quality of their work. Whether one's efforts led to great discoveries or not, everyone received the same compensation. The results of research work depended on the person himself, his potential and ability to work within the time constraints.

When I was a freshman, I naively believed that faculty members who could not meet their goals had only themselves to blame. Soon I realized that the success of a person was often resented by those with lesser accomplishments.

*Finally, a
university student.*

Slowly we began to understand better these complicated relationships among the faculty. The envious unsuccessful teachers attempted to underestimate the importance of other people's work. These unhappy teachers were eager to harm the pride of a person as a family man, as a friend, as a teacher, as a scientist, as a leader, in order to compromise the successful one. Surrounded by such a bitter environment, the Dean had to leave his position and take a job elsewhere. Yet he was the only person with such a high academic degree. He was the department's only teacher with the highest doctorate degree and the lifetime title of "professor." Luckily for us, students, the departure process took two years.

Of course, I didn't spend my whole college life studying.

I was exposed to some very interesting people. As a member of University's volleyball team, I was deeply involved in sports. I also was fond of theater. When communicating with others, I felt that my knowledge of music didn't compare favorably, I started taking an evening course about music at the conservatory. For similar reasons I took an art course at a museum. My life was interesting and busy. I seriously tried to prepare myself for the next period of my life. It seemed to me that there were no barriers that I couldn't overcome on the way to my goal.

One thing kept me worried—money. I didn't have enough, especially for clothing.

When I was a freshman, I wore my soldier's uniform or a pair of trousers, a shirt, and a light jacket I purchased with money I saved during my time in the army. As a soldier I received three rubles a month. In December I was still wearing my light jacket with the sleeves pulled up. Noticing the cold temperatures, my friends tried to convince me that it was time to pull the sleeves down. Jokingly, I answered that I would not change my habits only because the weather was changing. The truth was that I was embarrassed when the sleeves were pulled down because they didn't cover my arms. I have very long arms and my height is 6'2." With each day my financial difficulties increased. It was difficult for me to provide enough food and an adequate wardrobe. I began to think about where and how I could earn more money.

I had passed the required university examinations for the first semester with the highest scores. These results provided a scholarship that had 25% more financial aid than the ordinary student. This still wasn't enough. Like many other students, I was not afraid to work. I tried many casual jobs. Often I went to the railway station to unload the commodity trains or worked in a vegetable warehouse. I spent some time as a insurance agent and as a tutor of math.

With my savings I was able to afford twenty-four days at a summer sports camp at the Black Sea, city of Odessa. That was a really happy time.

I was twenty-five years old. It was my first time that I ever saw the sea. I will never forget that first impression. The name "Odessa" was associated with many fine things – the sea, one of world's best opera houses, great architecture, and the special character of a community representing approximately fifty different nationalities. Hundreds of legends and jokes were created about the central market of the city named "Privoz."

Our camp was just fifty feet from the sea in one of the best parts of Odessa called "Chernomorka." At that time the camp had approximately three hundred students from Odessa and other cities of Ukraine, Moldova, China, and Vietnam. I excitedly looked forward to the rest, sports, literature, and musical events. It was the first time in my life when I really felt relaxed. I felt like my soul was balanced.

On the second day something happened that upset me. I was elected as the head of the camp's student council, and I had to carry out some new responsibilities. I was initially upset over this decision but soon calmed down. This responsibility didn't involve a lot of work. I previously had some experience as a leader. I was a youth organization leader both during the Army and at the University. I had already developed communication skills. I had the ability to put myself in the other person's shoes. I knew how important it was to try to understand the thoughts and reasons for the other person's behavior. I also knew to treat people with respect. I was able to lead the other students in a gentle manner. While respecting their personality and interests, I convinced the students that sometimes we all have the responsibility to do not only what we liked but what is necessary for the whole team. This was a significant part of the rules of our camp life.

To help me, I had active and wonderful assistants. One was a poet, another a philosopher, and still another was a great sportsman. I learned that people are more agreeable during vacations and it is easier to build good relations.

That summer in 1960, I met young people from the United States for the first time. At that time the relations between the USA and the USSR were extremely strained. With centuries of tradition behind us, our attitude towards foreigners was cautious. However, in this case they were not just foreigners but Americans. Moreover, they were possibly future specialists on Russia.

Our camp director and a KGB representative declared that we had to meet with these future American spies. We were prepared for a "friendly" meeting. We were told to be hospitable and to behave with pride. We were supposed to ask our guests as many questions as possible and thus limit their ability to ask us about our lives. Only if it were necessary were we allowed to give them our work address. At that time lots of people lived in cellars or semi-cellars. If an American student visited such a home in Odessa, the Soviet's social policies would be discredited. When playing sports with them the Socialists were to favor volleyball as we had a great team. Chess was another safe sport as it was not popular in the US and they would do badly. Finally, we were to stress ping-pong, a sport in which Chinese and Vietnamese students were the great masters. Clearly we had to show our superiority in everything.

One day this event went basically according to the plan,

with a few exceptions. First of all, there were informal talks between young, educated people. The informal conversations were to involve an exchange of opinions on many aspects of life as young people in two distinct social-economic systems. Of course, we had different opinions on many things. We were glad when we found that our points of view were similar. As we planned, we won the athletic competitions but could not reject the request of the guests to play basketball. The Americans won. That one day spent with Americans influenced our stereotype of Americans. We did not quickly change our views about the life style of Americans, but many of us began to think seriously about our attitudes.

One event had an even greater impact on us than our American encounter.

A student had missed a few days of camp and had returned only on the day of our meeting with the Americans. Because of this he was unaware of everything. Innocently, he turned the volume on his radio up very loudly. To make matters worse, he was playing American jazz, music that was forbidden at that time. The student started to sing along and with such passion that everyone at the meeting started to laugh.

However, the meeting administrators believed the student and some members of the student council had acted irresponsibly and ignored the political importance of the event. Each of us was punished. The "singer" was expelled from the University despite the fact that he had only graduated from the University two months before that unlucky day. It was said that he poorly represented the Soviet students. The administration made the student return his diploma to the dean's office. One year later, after many apologies and explanations, he finally got his diploma back.

During my sophomore year I continued to study with great enthusiasm. By that time my financial situation had improved. I began to work as a bookkeeper in one of the city's athletic clubs. My work schedule was good. I had to be in the club's office two afternoons each week plus one evening or part of a weekend. My life was in order, or it was until the trial of my friend, Leon Shurman.

Most of my college classmates were seventeen or eighteen years old, but there were older people among us. Some of them were married and had children. Since the students' scholarships were obviously not enough for living expenses, many students tried to earn extra money.

Leon started to work four hours a day as a lathe operator at a machinery company. His work hours were different from the University's lectures schedule. Eventually that company was inspected by the Ministry of Finance. Serious financial violations were found. Somebody reported Leon as one of the company's workers. This was a problem.

According to the law at that time, full time students were not allowed to work. It was considered a crime for a person to be getting a government scholarship and a salary as a worker. This information reached the Dean's office. In three days he was expelled from the Young League of Komsomol. This meant he would be automatically expelled from the University. Fellow students knew Leon's family situation; he had a wife and a little daughter. It was not difficult to imagine his financial situation. I decided to defend him.

I understood how financial reasons pushed Leon to take that job. It is not easy to work and study at the same time. It was a hard and wearisome schedule. Before Leon's predicament none of us second-year students knew that about the employment restrictions for full-time students. Not knowing the law, of course, did not release one from acting according to the law, but there should be fair treatment.

Upon closer examination, it appeared that Leon did not violate the law. The law specifically restricts full-time students from working full time. Leon was only working part time. Furthermore, his job did not affect his studies. He still was earning good grades and because of that he was continuing to receive financial aid. Regardless of whether Leon violated the law, I felt that expelling him from the University was too strict a punishment. Such a punishment would affect his whole life. I argued that it was not fair to expel him.

My statement shocked most of my teachers since my position was different from theirs. The Chief of the Department of Political Economics, Dr. Sidorov, stated that my statement was wrong, and that I was without principles or an unscrupulous person. People liked to pin labels on others. That was a serious accusation. It implied I was a man without principles! As I expected, I was punished later. I feared that with such a label I could not expect to have a respected job in future.

Leon was expelled from the University and drafted into the Army for three years. His life was torn apart. His wife left him forever and took their daughter. This affected his stability and self-confidence and probably influenced his career. For many years he appealed to different organizations explaining that he didn't do anything harmful. Finally, the fourth or the fifth committee to review his case found him not guilty.

Three years later he was reinstated as a university student and graduated successfully. However, he never received an apology from those "respected" teachers who classified him as a criminal.

There were different opinions about the speech I gave in

behalf of Leon. Only eight years later when we gathered together for a college reunion, I learned that most of my fellow students shared my opinion. We held college reunions every five years. I became the chairman of those gatherings. That is how my friends showed their attitude towards me and rewarded me for my behavior in a critical situation such as Leon's. But all that was later.

Step by step I was learning the reality of life in the academic world. Some aspects of this life were not always pleasant. By the beginning of my junior year at the university, I came to the conclusion that it was better to work full-time and take evening classes. That was not an easy decision since it took me five long years to overcome all the obstacles in the way of my becoming a college student. None of my relatives or friends shared my opinion. Nevertheless, I had personal reasons for my decision.

In my third year we primarily had lectures on professional subjects such as economics, finance, and accounting. To my great surprise I found that the technical college where I had studied for a year and a half gave me a practical understanding. My technical school's teachers might not have had a college education, but they had years of work experience in banks, enterprises, financial organizations, and industrial ministries. My college teachers had master's degrees but lacked work experience. Day by day I found that I already had learned most of what they were teaching in these subjects.

After what happened to Leon, I stopped working in the sports club, but still I needed extra money. My decision was also motivated by my understanding that more experience would help me get a better job upon graduation. I knew that my good grades would not be enough.

However, the primary reason was my commitment to my

professional future. My interest in science really began in 1960, my second year. By that time I knew that I wanted to devote myself to science. Many people thought I had special abilities for that field. I dreamed about research work.

That year the university was sponsoring a multi-republic conference on the new State program of improving agriculture with chemicals. As an active member of the student scientific society, I was asked to prepare and present a speech. I was immensely pleased. I read all the available literature on the topic. I also interviewed leading researchers of many departments and laboratories, as well as specialists in collective farms and farmers. They gave me many different answers. With this fund of information I was able to put together ideas portraying different aspects of the scientific issues and address practical needs. My report was said to be one of the best. Moreover, I was granted the honor to present my report to the final conference.

In total three reports were presented. The Chairman of the Conference was President of the University. Also present were deans, faculty chairmen, teachers, and students of several Universities.

It exceeded my expectations. Many people complemented my ability to conduct scientific research. After that conference I started to devote even more time to the student scientific society. One of my research subjects was the different scientific theories of management in the West. I was thinking seriously about my future in science.

However, two factors made me believe that the doors to a scientific institution would be closed to me. First of all, hiring priorities favored people of a particular nationality, and I was not one of those people. Also, I thought that my reputation was forever damaged by my "unsuccessful" statement defending Leon. I expected that I would be limited to an assignment in a small town. By that time I knew the social system well and was familiar with "the rules." I had no illusions. Nevertheless, I still had one chance to devote myself to science. I imagined that I could find a full-time job as an economist or a in the field of finance in a company and spend my free time after office hours to scientific work.

Back then research work was quite different. There was no Internet. The libraries of small towns were small and lacked specialized literature such as professional journals. Also, because of the town's size, there never were any professional conferences or seminars. Under such conditions it was hard to communicate with other professionals. To make my dream come true, I knew that I'd have to work in a populated area with good libraries. That was the reason I wanted to find a job in a big city.

Chapter 6

WORKING IN THE PLANNED ECONOMY

After many months of searching for a suitable job, I found one with a company that recycled scrap metal. I was hired as their labor economist. After eight months I was promoted to be Chief of the Company's Planning and Economics Department. I was surprised with my recommendation for a promotion. I had not thought about getting a higher position. There were people with considerably more seniority. Some had worked there for more than ten years. I also didn't want the promotion because it would interfere with my educational goals. Although I worked during the day, in the evenings I continued studying seriously at the University. Even a significant raise and additional benefits could not make me forget about my major goal of getting a good education. I explained my feelings to the President of the Company, Gregory Yakovlenko. However, he refused to find my reasons persuasive. He said that he needed a person with a fresh outlook and new ideas.

To make me even more interested, he put me on the a special privileged list enabling me to get an apartment quicker. Thousands of people had been on an apartment waiting list for ten years or more. In fact many of them worked for more than twenty years and were never granted an apartment. Having lived in barracks and dormitories and having rented rooms in private homes for ten years, I was naturallly attracted to his offer and eventually agreed.

Every year the Ministry of Economics (Gosplan) used to set up a schedule of wages for every government-owned company. These limits were supposed to cover all labor related expenses. In reality it was not sufficient to support the required production. From the first months of my work I tried to understand how the executive organization determined the appropriate pay.

At that time I was responsible for my company's labor organization and the workers' remuneration. After completing numerous and very detailed calculations, I found out that during the last three years no correlation could be between the work completed and the money paid for it. I knew also the wage fund that we should be getting for the next year. As I expected, we got an inappropriately low amount again. At least I thought so and reported that fact to the Company executives. I asked the Chief Executive to give me permission to represent our interests to the Gosplan. He agreed.

In response to numerous requests of a particular department of Gosplan to agree with their decision and sign necessary papers, I asked them to focus attention on the research I had given them. This debate had been ongoing for more then a month when the chief of this Department, Michael Fedder, invited me to a confidential meeting. He tried to persuade me that life was more complicated than mathematical calculations, and consequently I would have to accept their decision. My response was very simple: I would be more than happy to accept their decision if he would explain to the employees why they would not be getting the wages they deserve. Finally, I won. I subsequently learned that it was the first time that my company had successfully changed the opinion of the authorities. That was my first victory. I guess that is why I remember it so well.

My responsibilities were significantly enlarged. Before, I was responsible for issues concerning the organization of labor and remuneration. That was not easy work since it concerned the daily needs of the staff and mistakes were not forgiven.

My new functions included the development of annual and five year business plans relating to production, finance, industrial and technical issues, and standards. Additionally, I had to produce a corresponding business document which reported the actual results. An important part of my work was maintaining external contacts with Gosplan, Ministry of Finance, State Bank, and numerous Industrial Ministries.

It was an interesting and satisfying period of my career. I gained valuable experience. I learned significant details of the planning system and how complicated the work of an industry planning specialist can be. This enlarged my outlook and knowledge of the country's economic system.

I found that the tasks planned by Gosplan were inadequately supported by financial and technical resources. Gosplan treated the standards and specifications as being of secondary importance. Instead, planning was primarily based on the reported results achieved. If the plan was not completed by the company, the quota of the current year was the base for the next year's plans. As a result of such policy, usually over achieving companies hid their real productive potential, while others, under the pressure of the executives, overstated their output. The reason was simple. The local Party executives and the leaders of the many industrial ministries tried to impress the higher level executives. They wanted to appear as if they had great abilities and were hard working.

After Leonid Brezhnev died, Party General Yuriy Andropov, began a tough struggle against the false representation of production. However, he ignored the fact that the Communist Party and State executives were encouraging the false representation of data. While they were not able to achieve their budget, The government still reported that they did. It was not the actual production that was their priority, but rather the statement that each year productivity had increased.

Years later when I had close contacts with the key specialists of the National Gosplan, I understood how they prepared their five-year plan. I found out how the plan was debated and massaged until it met the demands of the country's highest Party leaders.

The Gosplan knew the plans were not accurate and not supported with necessary resources. The Industrial Ministries knew it too and struggled with the Committee for a plan reduction futilely. In the end the Ministries gave the unrealistic plans to the enterprises, farms, and companies. The enterprises tried to communicate to officials that these were unattainable targets and not a planning process at all. It was specifically at the enterprise and farm producing level that this caused the greatest pressure in practice. But no one was able to change the process. The enterprises had no choice but to find any way available, sometimes an unlawful way, to fulfill the plans.

I worked sixty hours a week. In addition, I attended classes four times a week, from 7:00 to 11:00 PM at the University.

During one of my evenings at the University, I met Mrs. Raisa Sharkova. She graduated from our faculty two years before and had begun to work as an assistant professor. We had known each other approximately three years by that time and treated each other with respect.

She mentioned that she would be changing jobs and planned to start working at the Institute of Economics of the Academy of Science. She would be working under Professor Makeenko who had established and then became chief of a new department there.

I congratulated her and jokingly told her that when she became a "big boss," she should not forget to invite me to work for her.

Soon, I received a message to call Professor Makeenko. I called the professor. He asked me about my life, my salary, my chances for getting an apartment, and many other things. Then he described a possible job position at the Academy of Science. He explained that I would need to forget about getting an apartment for a few more years. Furthermore, I would need to accept a lower salary; it would be forty percent less than what I was being paid.

He advised me to mail him the necessary application papers, and he would do his best to help me to get the job.

This opportunity is what I had been dreaming about for years. However, I answered that I needed a couple days to think about the proposal.

At that time I was dating my future wife Valentine. We were planning our future together. Valentine, and her relatives did not want me to accept this new office, since it affected my opportunity to get an apartment. In spite of their feelings, I accepted the position.

However, it took another three months until Professor Makeenko could persuade the President of the Academy, the Chief of the Institute of Economics, the Human Resources department, and some of the institution's other leaders to give me the job.

While this delay was uncommon, so was the fact, that I, a Jew, was able to get a job position at the most prestigious research institution. Many people were surprised that I got this job. Considering it to be an exception to an "unwritten policy." Still, it was one of the greatest days in my life, even though the new job complicated my life.

When I began working for the Academy of Sciences, I was in my fifth year of college still attending evening classes. According to the law I should have four months free from work to prepare my graduation thesis. However, because I was new at my job, I realized that I had to work on my project after the office hours.

I felt motivated to do my best since I was surrounded by intelligent, talented, and experienced people. I wanted my performance to be comparable. However, at the end of the work day I had different thoughts. In spite of my exceptional shortage of time, almost every day I was *forced* to spend two or more hours playing volleyball.

One of the Academy of Science Vice-Presidents, Professor Borif Spasskiy, was fond of volleyball. Somehow he learned that I played for the University team. It happened that it was time for the annual city volleyball championship. Professor Spasskiy asked me to play on the Academy's team. How could I tell the "captain" of the team and the "captain" of the Academy of Sciences, as we called him, that I did not have time?

For five years, I had been getting excellent grades at the University and I wanted similarly to get an excellent grade on my thesis. I would expect nothing less.

All this also conflicted with the most important thing in life. I wanted to be with my beloved Valentine every day. For four months I only slept three to four hours a day. I had always worked a lot, but never like this.

What supported me at that time? A great spirit, positive emotions, and my determination to be successful. In a few months I was one of the university's two students to graduate with honor. My work schedule became manageable again.

For twenty-eight years, I worked for the Academy of Sciences. After my third year I presented my thesis and received a Ph.D. in Economics. Later I received my second, the highest, doctorate degree, and life-time title "Professor of Economics," published seven books and almost one hundred articles. In 1977 I received one of the most prestigious awards for my research achievements. Through my work experience I met people of different social levels from various regions of the country. I've always carried with me a sense of great respect and great gratitude for my most important teacher, Professor Makeenko. He opened the door to the world of science for me and gave me the opportunity to use my abilities. Almost everything else depended on my personal abilities.

Chapter 7

ROSES AND THORNS

Three quarters of my career, I worked in the field of economics. I aspired to be a scientist for two reasons. First, it was prestigious. Second, people who worked in science, especially those who were successful, were paid relatively well. With time I realized that these two factors became secondary. For many of us the special nature of science had become the primary factor.

One works fourteen hours a day not because somebody pushes him or because of good financial compensation but for something more important. The interest and commitment to scientific work and the professional recognition from colleagues become the driving forces.

Probably there is no realm other than science where the result of the work is so unpredictable and there is no other career where the result of one's work takes so long to be determined. But what incomparable happiness, what sense of self-satisfaction the scientist has, when the desired result is achieved at last! I had the pleasure of victories from hard work, financial prosperity, and the ups and downs of my career.

I will never forget that feeling of satisfaction when I saw my first published article in a magazine nor or that feeling of pride when my second article was recognized by professionals from Bulgaria.

In a small office there were five of us, my collaborators and me. There was a phone call and I answered it. Later, as my friends recalled, they noticed that my face started turning pale red, and then dark red. The Ministry of the Food Processing Industry of the USSR had invited me, a young and not very famous scientist, to give a speech at the All-Union conference. Nearly a month before that I had published the abstract of my Ph.D. thesis. According to the existing rules I sent one hundred copies to one hundred addresses. The specialists of the Ministry found it to be interesting enough to invite me to give a lecture to them and explain my new ideas in detail about industry improvement.

I had many more conferences and seminars in different regions as well as in foreign countries to look forward to. But that one was my first and unexpected invitation.

The publishing of my first book, "Quantitative and Qualitative Analysis of Manufacturing" was a great event in my life. The list also included scientific diplomas and certificates, the Award of the Academy of Science, and recognition one of my scientific works at the Exhibition of National Economic Achievements—the highest recognition of practical value of scientific research—and many others. While the work in science provided satisfying moments, there were also many problems—many of them.

After getting a Ph.D. in Economics, my first independent project was devoted to improvements in the utilization of the manufacturing work force. According to the system, working time lost in excess of thirty minutes was recorded. Anything less was ignored. The cumulative sum of these "less than 30 minutes" was significant.

I was the first one to develop and propose a simple and economical method to measure the amount of actual working time. Using this method we found that thirty-five percent of working time was unproductive. This was fifteen times more then official statistics claimed. I created a complex system of measures to reorganize the processes of production.

Based on that research I wrote a two-hundred page book, "Working Time". Everything was centralized and censored, especially anything that was published.

Publication had to be recommended by my Academy and also by two other institutions. Then the publishing house sent the manuscript to two or three additional reviewers. Any of these steps could block a books publication.

My book was discussed by the council of the Academy, where I worked, and was recommended for publication. I also received positive responses from the other reviewers. The only thing left before publishing was to get approval from the Food Processing Industry whose enterprises were the basis for this Project.

When I had the meeting with the department chief of planning and economics Isaac Komarov, I was finally told that the book would not be published. When I asked why, he answered that my book said that the managerial staff of companies and their ministers were incompetent. I tried to persuade him that I was not talking about the people but about a new method which allowed them to react quickly and effectively to problems in the work place. I had a few more confrontational meetings with Mr. Komarov, but my arguments were rejected. Instead of a book, a small brochure which described my new methodology was published. Because the honor of the bureaucrats was more important than the work for which they were responsible, I worked almost a year for nothing.

Five years later I received a project to analyze the work quality and the productivity of management staffs of seventeen different Ministries—large industry branches. I had to propose measures for improving the efficiency of their work.

Seven employees of my department and I spent six months working on the project.

Our final evaluation of work quality and productivity was negative. Technology and equipment had not been improved for years. If new technology was used in some rare cases, it concerned only small parts of manufacturing but had little or no effect on the total picture. Manufacturing costs were growing faster than productivity gains.

At the end of 1980s and early 1990s the word "stagnation" characterized the economy of the USSR. But "stagnation" only partly described the reality. The economy experienced a significant decline of quality, quantity, and profits. A program of financial, economic, and organizational measures were required to improve the situation.

We knew in advance that we were dealing with complicated circumstances. We were also dealing with people with power and lots of contacts. We realized that any criticism of them would be painful, and they would be very defensive. Every single step in our research was checked many times. The reliability of the information we used and the final results and conclusions could be checked by the industrial professionals themselves. For this purpose we provided them with special instructions and mathematical schemes.

The analysis covered a three year period for seventeen branches of industry. There was little to question about our methods.

It seemed that we had finished our work. But we did not understand adequately the "wisdom" of bureaucrats.

The leaders of the seventeen industries that we studied

ignored the results of this project without comment, as if nothing had happened.

I decided to answer their reaction with the only "weapon" that a scientist has. I wrote an article that was published in a newspaper in a few days. Those who worked in industry, as well as the general public, could learn a lot from this article. A newspaper article's life is only one day. But that was not possible with this article.

Some people were indignant for a long time after, while others tried unsuccessfully to prove that the results of our study were wrong. This Project and the article brought only trouble for me. Some people, including my wife, told me that I could be fired.

Over time my relations with the leaders of the industries improved, at least it seemed. I had sincere intentions. I merely tried to show the facts and to help improve the situation. Also I was the leader of two other Projects—Democratic Bases of Management and Product Quality Management of Industry. These projects maintained my relationship with these leaders.

While I was seriously busy with a new research topic, I still continued to develop additional aspects of the previous Project. After a couple of months I presented my expanded research to the highest State Planning Agency (Gosplan). My main idea was that in small republics such as Moldova, Estonia, Armenia, and Kirghizstan, Ministries were unessential units of management. I proposed a system of managing their economies without industrial Ministries. As one of my friends told me, the reaction to this work was like the "result of an exploded bomb."

I knew my proposal would affect the interests of many people. It was not difficult to guess the reaction of those with possible salary cuts and deprivation of privileges. I was now an experienced person who understood that this was a risky a step for me and that the Government and especially the Gosplan would criticize my reorganization proposal. I decided to do it anyway.

I truly believed in the necessity of such a reorganization. As life would prove in several years, not only the small but the big republics also reduced most of their Ministries.

By this time I had worked for the Academy of Science for fifteen years and developed dozens of projects which were successfully implemented. I was optimistic that my scientifically-justified recommendations would be accepted in spite of the negative personal impact on me from some of these powerful people. This was what I thought. In reality something improbable happened. There were no comments on whether to approve or disapprove my research, agree or disagree with the conclusions.

A few days later the First Deputy Prime Minister, who also was the Minister of Gosplan, Mr. Savochko, visited the Academy. Usually a person in such a position invited people to his office. He explained that he wanted to "debate" with me in front of my coworkers. I was somewhat aware of this man's past career and personality, and knew he would not tolerate any threat to his control.

He was arrogant and self-satisfied, a short, stocky man who was proud to have served in the Navy. People called him "our little Napoleon."

He had worked in the inspection department of an engineering factory, where he judged the quality of goods for military purposes. He was not the best professional, but he curried favor with the Communist leaders until they started paying him attention. Soon enough, he was promoted.

For a short time he became President of the factory, then

Party Secretary (leader) of the city Beltsy, then Chief Department Head of the Central Committee of the Communist Party. Finally he was made First Deputy Prime Minister.

It was not easy to work with this man. He considered the word of the Party not only the law, but the supreme authority. When people asked him why, he responded that sometimes you can break the law, but the orders of the Party must always be followed. He, of course, gave the orders, and people disliked him intensely.

He especially hated scientists because they tried to provide him with analytical reports, new ideas, and sometimes critical notes about the economy. He was opposed to all scientists and adjusted his standards so that he could ignore them. And now I would be forced to discuss my ideas with him.

He said, "I did not read your books so I don't know your view about the economy and its future."

I replied,"That's not my fault."

"Your last report really startled me, and I hope you understand why I visited the Academy."

"I offered a new idea that could make radical changes in the management of the economy. Shouldn't it be seriously discussed?"

From the very beginning , it became clear to me and my coworkers that he was going to punish me for my "politically incorrect" work and at the same time to scare the others in attendance.

There was a serious exchange of opinions. I tried to answer all of his questions and remarks professionally and give the necessary explanations of my recommendations. Other people had the same opinion. Even Savochko admitted that I tried to explain everything scientifically.

He said that I could be right in some details, but in general it was unconstitutional work. Also he wondered whether, if there were no Ministries, the Cabinet of Government would have nothing to rule. Everyone was silent, each of them understood that it was the end of my career. With such a label no one would ever employ such a person, especially in the fields connected with science.

This happened in a country where everything belonged to the state, and all income was dependent on the government. If a person had savings, there was enough for only three or four months of living. I felt I was professionally ruined.

In an instant I forgot about science and my research plans. The only thing that was on my mind is how I could support my family. I had good acquaintances, people who knew my professional qualities. There were close friends who normally would be happy to help. But in this situation nobody would take such a risk. I was totally demolished. I continued to go to my office but could not focus on my work. I thought about calling some people, but I refused to put them in an awkward position. The only thoughts I had were about what happened and why I failed. Though in reality the reasons were very clear.

Everything was closely aligned with the politics of the country, including science. Even chemistry, physics, and biology could not escape that influence. History, philosophy, economics, literature, ethnography were under strict Party supervision and influence.

I blamed myself. I was naïve. I should not have forgotten where I worked. Since I was a Jew, it was a fluke to be employed by the Academy of Science in the first place. I should have remembered who controlled our work and what social and political people surrounded me.

Soon my boss, the Academician Nicolas Phrolov, invited me to talk. It so happened that we started work at the Academy at the same time. There was only one little difference. He came in as the President, while I, still a student, was employed as a laboratory assistant.

By now I was Chief of one of the three large departments. I had been working with Dr. Phrolov all these years. As an employee I had endeavored to be professional, a hard worker, witty and skillful, and I believed I fulfilled all these attributes. However, I had never been, I thought, among his close friends, and instead tried to keep a particular distance.

People who worked there and many others outside the Academy knew his authoritarian and rough personality. And I knew his "friendship" with people did not always end up being good for them.

Dr. Phrolov had devoted three decades to this endeavor. He was a well-known specialist in theoretical economics. The Academy worked primarily on issues of practical economics. This was the reason for periodic professional disagreements. He was a very powerful person. He had support from high-ranking government people. He worked for them primarily and pushed us to work in that direction as well. For him, as for other leaders in all fields, the word of the Communist Party was law.

I did not expect anything good from our conversation that day. My situation was very tenuous. Even if he could assist me, he would not risk his relations with the government. With such thoughts in my mind, I went to that meeting. I had never before come to his office with such anxiety.

The conversation was very laconic, "We have a lot of work to do. I have protected you." The words "I have protected you" meant that he had discussed my case with people, who were above Savochko in the government hierarchy.

He did something very extraordinary. I have always been thankful to him for this. At the same time I tried to understand his motives. The only rationale I could think of was that he needed me as his employee.

In academia people were employed not only because of their professional qualities but because of their nationality and relationships with the powerful people. In those institutions many relatives (especially wives and children) and some acquaintances of the Party bosses or representatives of the Government were first to be employed. Poor placements were inevitably made. An experienced person in manufacturing or agriculture does not necessarily adapt to scientific work. The Academy had a lot of projects to accomplish in spite of many "misfits" in its workforce. Dr. Phrolov obviously needed a group of people who he could rely on. I guess I was one of these people.

I worked at the Academy twelve more years. I learned from this experience and I became more cautious. If I had the opportunity to choose one of two projects such as one for the Government and the other for industry or agriculture, I always choose the latter. I preferred to work on long-term projects, since such work provided a greater opportunity for creativity. Also it did not impact the current interest of government people. If I had to choose whether to lead a project or be just a participant, I gave the leadership to someone else. To survive, I had to adjust to the conditions. Of course, such defensive behavior was not the way for a scientist to make the best impression. But those were the "rules of the game."

Soviet astronauts were the most celebrated and honorable group of people. Yet one of them answered a question, relating to this "delicate" situation in the country, he gave a piece of advice to others: "Do not go with the stream of life, do not go against the stream, just do your part of your job quietly."

These work experiences would not be of interest if it concerned only me, one person or a small group of people. However thousands of Soviet Union scientists could give you many similar examples of Party science supervision. Everything was important to those supervisors, except science itself.

I loved my work like I love a rose, but the way I had to approach it was like a thorn.

Chapter 8

KGB:

The All-Seeing Eyes and the All-Hearing Ears

The KGB was the government security organ in the former USSR and it was the most infamous institution inside and outside the borders of the nation. Much is associated with its limitless power, cruelty, subterfuge, rudeness, torture, death, fanaticism, bravery, professionalism, insult, anonymity, bribery, twisted facts, treason, and involuntary confession. Dozens, maybe hundreds, of epithets could be used to describe this mighty organization, but the one word that comes most readily to mind when one hears those three letters—KGB—is fear.

Hundreds of thousands of people gladly and loyally collaborated with this organization, often paying for it with their lives or the lives of their closest relatives and friends. Hundreds of thousands of people worked with the KGB not because of a desire to do so, but because of their circumstances. Millions of others tried to steer clear as much as possible from it. But it was difficult to protect oneself and escape the all seeing eyes and the hearing ears of KGB.

Even in my first year at the University, I suspected that some of my acquaintances were KGB agents. Later I understood that such agents were to be found everywhere. They could be present in any organization and in any formal or informal gathering. The KGB penetrated every component of society. Coming in contact with this organization was easy. Escaping it was almost impossible, especially for those who received professional recognition in industry, arts, or sciences. I could not escape it either.

In 1972, when I had a senior position at the Institute of Economics at the Academy of Science, I was invited to appear at the city's military registration office. I didn't attach much meaning to this summons since these meetings occurred frequently to reflect changes in one's professional career or as a reserve officer. This latest summons to headquarters seemed to me a necessary formality.

I was frequently reassigned to different divisions in case of war or a promotion in rank. I served three years in the Army. I never attended military school, but I was a good sergeant. My education was splendid too. For those years of service, I achieved the rank of 2nd lieutenant. I never thought about a military career. After demobilization I devoted myself wholly to civilian life and never gave a minute to military business.

Nevertheless, upon becoming an academic, I received elevations in military rank, and when I became a Captain in the reserves, my friends jokingly, advised me to seriously mull over whether I could have a bigger career as an academic or as an officer.

I arrived at the appointed place and time. I was warmly greeted and received apologies that the meeting would take place slightly later in a different building. When I arrived at the indicated office, I noticed that the man behind the desk was busy doing something with the desk drawer, and something wasn't working out quite right for him.

He invited me to sit and introduced himself as Michael

Ivanov, a member of the KGB. I was invited to this office because it was the most convenient place for this sort of meeting. Soon, I realized I was dealing with a smart and experienced man.

What made me most wary was what was in the desk drawer. I saw some wires and it became clear that my every word was being recorded. I was on guard from the first, but now my attention tripled. Any mistake could cost me dearly.

I started telling him how I liked my job, that I had offers of higher, more responsible positions with a correspondingly higher salary and increased benefits, but I valued my present position as an academic and was not interested in anything else. This was the right tactic.

Finally, he asked if I was familiar with the term "industrial espionage" and if I would be interested in working in another country. I didn't expect this turn of events. I expected that he would ask me to work for them in some capacity but not that. Recovering, I answered that I was probably not the man they needed.

First, even before the proposition, I reiterated that I liked my job, and had also become successful doing it.

Then he asked, "What if the nation needs it?" If my knowledge of economics was helpful, I answered, I would be ready to do whatever was needed of me. But if my understanding of 'industrial espionage' was correct, then it was first and foremost 'engineering' espionage, and I had no technical knowledge. My qualities obviously would not meet the needs of such a responsible position.

With steel in his voice he said that I could gain necessary knowledge for this job in three or four months.

The meeting ended amicably. He asked me to think about the offer and gave me his telephone number where I could reach him at any time, day or night. I never called him.

In the 1970s the head of the Communist Party at the Academy of Science was a deputy department head of the Central Committee of the Communist Party of Moldova and had previously been a significant employee of the KGB. This was a lofty position; the fate of thousands of scientists depended on him.

One day he gathered a group of scientific lecturers and asked us to prepare a series of lectures on an anti-Israel theme. Each of us was obliged to meet no less than ten times with an industrial, agricultural, or professional group on this subject. Some took this project to heart. Not only did they read the lectures but also secured time on radio and television to expose the "devious and racist" character of Israel and published articles and books on that theme. Some managed to make a career out of this, becoming popular personalities in certain circles. Honesty and objectiveness were not important.

I was totally opposed. But I was in an impossibly difficult situation. Saying openly that you would not submit to the will of the party boss and participating in these evil lectures meant losing all that you have attained. Agreeing was also not an option since it was contrary to my conscience as a human being and scientist. In my view this would be a betrayal of the memory of my forefathers. How could I even look at my wife, my son, and my friends after that?

I chose a third way. I kept quiet for a long time, but after another reminder of this new duty, I set up an appointment with the party boss.

I tried explaining to him that I do not know the language, culture, traditions, and Jewish religious rites, although I spoke Yiddish from childhood and knew to some extent the culture and traditions of our people. I often give lectures, but this is a special case. I cherish my professional authority and don't want to be an ordinary dilettante. Further, I presented him with my idea.

I could prepare a reference on the economic situation in Israel, comparing it with the economic situation in southern regions of the USSR; other lecturers could probably use this material.

Not waiting for his response, I remarked that of course it would be reasonable only in this situation, the comparison would be in favor of our country.

In two or three days, I called the office of the party secretary and indicated I was powerless to produce anything, since the analysis showed that the important agricultural yields in Israel, e.g. the production of milk per cow, was about twice that of our region.

For three years this experienced KGB person watched my every step and spoke out against promotions or any sign of recognition of my good works. Finally, a number of researchers helped him become a Ph.D. in Economic Sciences, and this newly minted 'scientist' got a significant promotion and moved on to another institution.

Many years passed. In the early 90s I met one of the active members of the anti-Israel campaign. He blurted out that I had acted wisely in refusing to participate in that political scheme. I told him I couldn't judge whether it was wise, but I was sure I had acted decently. He looked tired and glum. His face showed traces of recent beatings. This was in Vienna, Austria, where some immigrants from the former USSR heading for permanent residency in the USA or Israel. They decided to "thank" this learned and "principled" man for his "tireless" work.

I have already mentioned that I often gave lectures. I was regarded as a good lecturer. My audiences were workers in industry, agriculture, building, factory managers, ministers and assistant ministers, and leaders of regions.

I was often invited to meetings with foreign tourists to acquaint them with the general economic situation of the country and the region.

At one of these meetings with tourists from the USA, one woman unexpectedly expressed her wish to speak to me privately as an economist on a personal matter. I replied that I would be delighted to try and answer her question but I asked the official translator to take part in the conversation. I knew that Intourist employees, including translators, were in close contact with the KGB. The presence of the translator freed me of any future explanations about why I spoke one on one with a foreigner and what we discussed.

My caution was well founded. It would be difficult to extricate oneself from any suspicions.

The foreigner, in good Russian, told me that she intended to stay in the USSR.

When I asked what prompted her to take such a serious step, she explained to me that she was born in the U.S., but her parents had come from Russia a few decades ago from the city of Samara on the Volga. Her husband had died recently and numerous misfortunes befallen her. She admitted that she had no relationship with her children and didn't get along with the neighbors. She wanted to know whether I could help her transfer her savings of about $80,000 from the USA to the USSR without major losses. It took some time for me to recover from this sudden request. Finally, I simply admitted to her that I was not a specialist in that field of economics. I emphasized that the question was not only economic but political. I suggested she discuss the question with more competent people. The only people who could set up such a meeting were the head of the Intourist company and the translator.

That evening I told my family of this remarkable event. That was something to wonder about. So many people are looking for ways to leave this country, and here is a puzzling desire of an American citizen to immigrate to the USSR.

The next day I had a planned meeting with specialists of the Ministry of Economics in their building. My departmental colleagues knew the phone numbers where I could be reached. At approximately 10:00AM they called me and informed me that the head of the First Department of the Academy was eager to locate me.

Any savvy person in the USSR knew that the First Department was essentially the undivided structural subdepartment of any enterprise, ministry, or organization consisting of professional workers from the KGB working on its behalf. The very name, "First Department" spoke of the role and aim of this entity.

I knew the head of this department by sight since his office and my department were located in the same building. We exchanged greetings, but I had no other contact with him. I was surprised that I was urgently needed by him. I asked my colleagues to give him the message that I off site working with a group of officials at the Ministry of Economics and that I would drop by his office after lunch.

As soon as I came into his office, he immediately asked, "What happened at that lecture of yours?"

"It was a lecture-like lecture," I replied. "I don't think anyone was dissatisfied."

"What about the woman who is trying to stay in the USSR?" He was obviously irritated that I had not told him about the incident. Apparently I had put him into a difficult spot, since instead of relaying what happened to his superiors, he had been informed of it by a third party.

I remarked that truly this was a unique event, but that evening I didn't attach any particular significance to it. I attempted to tell him in detail about my conversation with the tourist, reminding him that the translator also took part.

He interrupted me, saying that he had only one question: "What do you think? Was this woman a psychologically stable person?" There were some magazines on his desk, and I was able to divert my eyes from him for a few seconds.

This man, who had served them for decades, did not understand that with his one question he had fairly commented on the social structure of the entire country more accurately than any dozens of pages specifically prepared on that question by "foreign intelligence."

It appears that even in those far off times KGB operatives thought that only a mentally unstable person would come up with the idea of trading American citizenship for Soviet. For a long time among my closest colleagues and friends, the phrase "Is this woman psychologically stable?" became commonplace as a daily greeting or a question about how things are going.

In 1975, while I was in my forties, I went abroad as a tourist for the first time in my life. To be more specific, I visited two countries: Romania and Yugoslavia. The opportunity to go abroad was an extraordinary event for Soviet people and my wife and I were lucky to get permission for such a trip. We prepared for it carefully over a long period of time. Sometimes it even seemed to me that waiting gave us as much joy as the trip itself. Every city and especially every country had hundreds of unique places and things that would amaze travelers. We were looking forward to new adventures.

Our first stop was Bucharest, the capital of Romania. An interesting incident occurred there. On the first day the leader of group could not find one member, a woman. She came back in the evening and apologized, saying that she had gotten lost from the group and could not find her way in the city. Her name was Maria. In the morning the leader reprimanded here explicitly and indicated in no uncertain terms that if this happened to anybody else, the violator would be sent back to the Soviet Union from the Soviet embassy. We forgot her as Maria seemed to be a very nice and sincere person although a bit undisciplined.

A big, beautiful city, Bucharest captivated us with its architecture, the museum of the king's place, and numerous restaurants where in the evening the famous actors sang and danced. We remembered the city Brashov where there was one of the best European ski resort in the Carpatians, the city Sinia with the richest collection of tableware and glass and many other things in the country.

Yugoslavia seemed to us an incredible country because of the style of life. This semi-socialist, semi-capitalist country was in its best time during these years. As one of my friends said, the Yugoslavians accepted seriously only those socialist ideas which did not interrupt their capitalist prosperity.

In Belgrade, the capital, we saw for the first time stores where everything was in surplus amounts. You just bought what you wanted!

Comparing the constant deficit of everything in our country gave us the impression of one of the seven wonders of the world.

In Sarajevo we saw the notorious crossing where Archduke Francis Ferdinand, heir to the Austria-Hungarian throne, was assassinated in 1914 by a group of Serbian nationalists, who belonged to an organization known as the Black Hand. That was the event that marked the beginning of the World War I. And the Adriatic Sea! On the entrance to a popular city in that resort these words were cut into the rock, "If there is a paradise in the world, it is Dubrovniki."

Everything would have been great except one circumstance. In our group were people with different interests, but nobody had a right to spend even an hour as he or she wanted. In the historical museum in the republic of Chernogoria, one of six in Yugoslavia, I found a unique historical document.

During the Russian-Japanese War in 1904 Chernogoria was an independent country and had friendly relationships with Russia. Later on it lost independence as a country and became a part of Yugoslavia. However, they had not yet smoothed out their relations with Japan. In 1975 I found an official paper that indicated that Chernogoria, though about 7000 miles away from Japan, had been at war with Japan since 1904. I asked the leader of our group if I could stay for one more hour at the museum. He said he did not think the KGB representative would treat that as a thoughtful decision.

The KGB representative! All of us understood that there was such a person among us. Who was that? We had traveled eight days by that time, but we could not imagine who it was. We ruled out every person of whom we were suspicious.

While we were walking one evening along the riverbank, somebody started to sing Russian songs. Eventually we saw the man who was singing. He introduced himself as a retired colonel who fought as a partisan with Josev Tito. Some time ago he studied in a military college in Russia and knew Russian language and culture. Out of respect for our country, he invited some of our group to a restaurant. Such generosity amazed us, but suspecting something suspicious, my wife and I and two other couples declined the invitation from the beginning. Some other people agreed to accept. We learned later that this " colonel" was helping the KGB representative in our group get information about how we all behaved abroad.

Our twelve days voyage abroad was soon over. We got a lot of new impressions and new knowledge about life and made new friends. Only one thing remained unknown: the identity of the KGB agent who could hide so well.

About a year and a half later my wife, a dentist, met Maria, the woman who was with us during that trip, in her hospital. They were glad to meet again. They reviewed the trip. Maria then said that she was the KGB agent in our group and that she had given us a good report. She said my wife and I were perfect during that trip. With a smile, she added that such behavior itself was suspicious!

Chapter 9

CULTURAL DIVERSITY

I have always liked traveling. Trips that introduced me to new places, fresh perspectives, interesting people, and previously unknown lifestyles have been singularly enriching.

Since childhood I have remembered a practice followed by Peter Tretyakov. He was one of the most educated people of his time and a great art collector. In the latter half of the 19th Century, he established a private museum of Russian art and later gave the City of Moscow his priceless collection of paintings. The Tretyakov Gallery is one of the best museums of art in Moscow and to this day bears his name. He studiously prepared for his voyages and carefully planned them. The starting point of his annual travels was the last city or town of the previous year's trip. As a child I fantasized that someday I would be able to follow his example. But dreams and reality are two different things. Still, I had been to the United States before I became a resident, a number of European countries, and traveled throughout the fifteen republics of the former USSR, where there was much to see.

Imagine the conglomeration that was the USSR: a nation consisting of not only Russia, Ukraine and Belorussia but

90

numerous other countries with diverse cultures, religions, customs and traditions. These countries included Poland, Romania, Turkey, Iran, Afghanistan, Mongolia, and a dozen others, each unique. There was little in common between an Estonian and a Tadjik, a Moldovian and an Armenian and so on and so forth. Before the dissolution of the USSR, Americans for the most part associated it with Russia or what a traveler managed to see in Moscow, St. Petersburg, and a few other cities. In reality it was quite different.

Russia and the Newly Independent States (NIS) no longer compose a unified country. Actually there never was such a thing. Today there are fifteen independent nations, each with its own idiosyncrasies. Each has different language, culture and traditions. People of the USA comprise a huge number of nationalities. Here one can find representatives of all nations of the world. But the situation in USA is different. America has welcomed and continues to welcome everyone, but no one in America has a claim on territory of the country. The process of settling the territories of the former Soviet Union has gone on for centuries even millennia. The culture and customs of the people, their traditions, and rites have deep roots. Only the communist party leaders thought that this heritage could be taken out by the root in two or three decades. Life is much more complicated than this. Traditions and customs of a people are alive; they establish a base for their world view and life. Here are some examples I took away from my travels.

Kazakhstan

In Kazakhstan, I was almost 3000 miles away from home, the farthest that I had ever been. I was one of thousands of young people participating in Program No. 1 of the USSR in the 1950's. The purpose was the acquisition of virgin and fallow lands that had not been cultivated for centuries. In Kazakhstan, as in other countries, there are cities, museums, schools, scenic spots, sports centers, and much more. Outwardly, life here seemed similar to other regions, but there was much to be amazed by.

The endless steppe made the biggest impression on me. How many mysteries was it hiding? It was in Kazakhstan I became convinced that it's easier to get lost in the steppe than in the woods. The government, forgetting the needs of the enormous agrarian sector in Central Russia, Ukraine, and Belorussia, bestowed upon Kazakhstan virtually unlimited financial, material, technical, scientific, and labor resources with the aim of creating in the shortest amount of time a second breadbasket, after Ukraine. Day and night echelons of people and resources arrived. The best specialists were sent here from all regions of the nation. Leonid Brezhnev headed the program. It was after this "successful" undertaking that he rose two or three steps in the party hierarchy.

The living conditions were new to me. Drinking water was trucked in cisterns since the water wells were about 100 miles from us. In Ukraine in every population center there were wells about fifty to seventy meters apart. As for the quality of the water, don't mention it. During the day we suffered from the heat. At night we covered ourselves with whatever was at hand to keep warm. It was not only us, all who came here for six months or a year to work lived in tents. A significant portion of the native population lived in portable dwellings, the so-called yurtas.

Today Kazakhstan is renowned as a country with huge reserves of oil, gas and mineral resources. It's also known as a major component of the Soviet Union's space program.

According to some polls American companies rate this country as having the best business potential in all of the former soviet republics. But fifty years ago Kazakhstan was a country with a weak economy, a region just developing industry and with big hopes of becoming the most important producer of agricultural products in the USSR.

Unfortunately, Nikita Khrushchev's projects to transform agriculture radically in this region failed. After bumper crops of 1955 and 1956 the harvests significantly declined and failed to be as productive. Many decisions were made subjectively. Scientists-agrarians of the country didn't account for many factors, especially in the assessment of the quality of land. Leaders and specialists in agriculture easily submitted to party pressure, mainly to pressure from Khruschev. Investments in Kazkhsatan so strained the nation as a whole that for decades afterward the country could not help the traditional agricultural regions, especially in central Russia.

This program and its consequences were probably the chief reason for the stagnation of agriculture in the USSR. At that time we did not think about it. Moreover, we were young. We enthusiastically worked and truly believed that while working on electrification or on a cornfield, we were part of a great, historic event.

But people who worked here were smart, educated, and experienced, on one hand, and young, on the other. They were like me at the time—energetic but not understanding the crux of the matter. For the majority of us this enterprise was our first job. But unlike the older generation we interacted more with the native population. From these interactions we learned many interesting, enlightening things.

Even in high school I knew that in Kazakhstan,—poet improvisers—were highly honored. They made a huge contribution to the culture of their people. And now I was in a small hall, listening with a particular delight to one of the most famous of them. What is amazing was not only his special ability to improvise on any subject in lyrical scheme but also his instantly created works of epic nature and particular syntax. In Kazakhstan literacy based on the Russian alphabet appeared not long ago. And suddenly it was discovered that the widely-read folk poet could not read or write and knew little or nothing of Russian or European literature. It seemed to me that we witnessed this sort of contrast everywhere and in everything.

During the Soviet regime many changes took place in this republic. Schools, universities, and theaters appeared. Educational and cultural levels of the population increased significantly. The indigenous population began to give way to Russians and other nationalities. Outwardly, it appeared that relations between people here did not differ much from other regions of USSR. But interaction with Kazakh often revealed what at that time seemed remarkable to me.

The conglomeration of various clans with their individual outlooks and convictions and their battles in behalf of their interests were sometimes defining factors in the life of society. This discovery so amazed me that for many years afterwards I could not reconcile myself with it. Living in the twentieth century by laws of birthright, it was not even partially possible for me. In 1991 when Kazakhstan became an independent, free nation, many old traditions, including birthright and clan relations, were revived in the laws by the new government.

A few times I was a guest of Kazakh families. Nowhere and never again did I encounter hospitality such as this. When a dinner was served, everyone sat on the floor. Observing the traditions of the people I tried to fold my long legs so I wouldn't interfere with others. I noticed that as a guest, I was served the more savory dishes and even the bread is of better quality than the one that the hosts are having. They explained to me that these are the ways of a hospitable people. I tried to convince the hosts that this put me in an uncomfortable situation. It seemed to me that nearly everywhere in the world everyone at the table would have the same food, but my pleas fell on deaf ears. This was the custom, and it had to be followed.

Many years passed but I fondly remember these plain and industrious people from far-off Kazakhstan. It's with a particular delight that I relate to a people who managed to maintain many wonderful traditions, including their unique and charming hospitality customs.

Uzbekistan

It is ancient, beautiful, rich in people and resources. In terms of natural resources, Uzbekistan is one of the world's ten richest countries. Ninety-five percent of all minerals known to humanity are found here. It is the third largest producer of natural gas in the former soviet republic and has the fourth largest deposits of gold in the world. It was the Soviet Union's principal cotton producer.

I lived there for two years, served in the army there, and have visited numerous times. I read a lot about Uzbekistan, maintained contacts with people for years, and tried to be informed about events in the region.

The first nations in this territory appeared as long ago as the 8th century before the Common Era. The armies of Alexander of Macedonia were here. Ancient, fabulous cities like Samarkand, established 2300 years ago, Bukhara, Kokand, Fergana, and dozens of other, less well-known cities are rich in history, as well as the Capital city of Tashkent, amaze the imagination of anyone who visits them.

I've known many interesting people from Uzbekistan. Once, I was introduced to a renowned actress, a woman in her later years by then. She was famed in no small part due to her decision to appear on stage without a veil. It was a truly courageous act at that time. To go against centuries of tradition, to withstand disapproval, insults, and even death threats from friends, strangers, and even relatives took courage and strength of character. This woman had both.

I knew Zuchra Alimova, a young Ph.D. and Doctor of Philosophy in the USSR. The doctor was a thirty-five year-old Uzbek woman. This woman possessd a special mind and was also especially wise. This rare combination of youth and wisdom delighted those who had the opportunity to work with her or interact with her socially. Through my work I had many colleagues from the academic field as well as from business.

Yet, this is the East and in the East it's sometimes not easy to understand the true meaning of words or differentiate reality from perceived actions.

I was told of some honest, courageous people who in the so called Cotton Affair (1984) waged a hard and risky battle against Mr. Rashidov.

Mr. Rashidov, the Party leader of the republic, and his cohorts organized an underground system of manufacture and siphoned off government finances to the benefit of a select group of people. For ten years hundreds of enterprises and thousands of people worked exclusively for Rashidov and those like him. The scale of the theft and the unwillingness of leaders in Moscow to stop this illegal practice and punish the guilty parties shocked the Soviet society.

As long ago as the 1970s I was told there were entire settlements in the country where people lived in conditions of slavery. I could not believe it; I couldn't even imagine such a thing. But in the 1980s it was written in the newspapers. In a population of millions of people it was difficult to find someone who was indifferent to this question. When I asked why those who knew about it kept quiet for so long, I was given a convincing answer. They kept it to themselves because they feared becoming a slave themselves.

When I was in the military, there were episodes in which soldiers, guarding military installations would disappear without a trace. Search parties could not uncover anything. It was supposed that the local extremists were willing to commit any crime for a Kalashnikov rifle.

On weekends, some of us were given leave to go to the city and spend time as we saw fit. When a soldier found himself outside the gate of the military unit, he could not get enough of the air of freedom. Sometimes his actions were unrestricted. It was even harder to leave this "freedom" and return to the unit.

On a warm evening young people were taking a stroll, going to the movies or the theater, spending time with friends. If you were a soldier, you had to leave the city by 9: 00 PM so that by 10:00PM you could be back at the base about three miles away. I know that on many occasions I was lucky to return in time.

The military town was on the highway. Often the drivers would give soldiers a lift to the base as favor as their sole chance to return to the unit on time.

On one of these evenings we were clearly running late. My friend Victor and I decided that we could cover the distance in thirty-five to forty minutes if we ran. Another friend, Michael, decided to hitchhike. After ten or fifteen minutes we heard the rumble of a truck behind us. The driver would not stop for us. We noticed that Michael was in the back of the truck sitting with some other people. He even waved to us as if to say "I got lucky and you fools jumped the gun." No one saw him ever again. He disappeared without a trace.

Although it had been approximately forty years since Soviet rule had been established, some in the local population disliked Russians, including in their minds Latvians, Moldovians, Tatars, and soldiers of all ninety nationalities that were not indigenous to the area.

I've been to the city of Fergana many times. It's not large but cozy, beautiful, and rich with a past in its own particular image. Many years have passed, but I still remember a simple event that happened in that city.

A friend and I were on leave but we did not have much money. We were walking past a house. The house did not particularly interest us, but its orchard did. The peaches growing there were begging to be eaten. The woman who owned the house was sitting by the door, and we spoke to her. We hinted that we would like to taste some of the fruit in her orchard before we purchased any. All over the country, people treated soldiers with pity sometimes because they understood the hard lot of a soldier in the army. In this instance however, we surmised that we would have to pay for them. My friend and I checked our finances and came up with a little over a ruble. We asked how many peaches we could get with our ruble. "Ten," she replied. We bargained with her, but the woman firmly stood by her price. My friend announced his agreement but asked if we could pick the fruit ourselves and she agreed.

In the orchard, we picked the choicest fruits and at the same time sampled some of the peaches. Having eaten our fill, we left the orchard. We showed her the ten peaches we picked and offered her our ruble. Smiling, she refused to take the money, and suggested we give the fruit to our fellow soldiers. That startled us. Returning to the unit, we spoke about this amusing event and later forgot about it. Through the years I occasionally remember this woman with a kind heart and stern manner.

After I came to the United States, I did some research on the city of Fergana. Looking through the information, I was shocked. It appears that in the late 1950s, when I served in the Army, Fergana was the site of the first congress of fundamentalist Moslems demanding eradication of American and European culture as the aim of the organization.

Fergana! That was the city of my military youth and, I loved it. I am convinced that there are more people like the wise women with a kind heart there than people wishing the demise of modern civilization.

Georgia

Of all former republics Georgia held a special place in the USSR. With its generous, long summers, a warm sea, breathtakingly beautiful mountains, the rich vegetation of the subtropics, entertainment, and hospitality. Their love of country and their hospitality were legendary.

According to popular legend, God decided to give each people a piece of land. To declare his intentions, he gathered representatives of all nations to him. Everyone showed up on time, but the Georgians were late; they showed up after God had already distributed all the land. God was cross with the Georgians, and to the question as to why they were late, he was told the following answer, that they were delayed because they had guests and couldn't interrupt the ritual of hospitality, which they greatly respected. God accepted this explanation, but all the lands were already given away. Then God remembered that there was one piece of land left he was going to keep for himself, and he gave it to the Georgians. Since it was going to be God's own land, the best of everything could be found there: the sea, rivers, mountains, rich soil for growing tea, citrus, grapes, fruits and vegetables, and grains. Yet the chief wealth of the country is its peoples ancient traditions and their particular love of life.

I've been to Georgia dozens of times, and have met many people for professional reasons or socially, I had many acquaintances and made good friends. Workers and captains of industry, students and academics, doctors and geologists. Men and women, young and old. No matter what the situation or whom I met, I first and foremost saw a proud people. No matter what the material or work situation was, a Georgian always had a sense of dignity, pride in self and country, and love of anything associated with Georgia. This gave me a great feeling of respect for them.

Many times, I was at the banquet table of a Georgian family. How richly and beautifully they entertained their guests! But each guest also had to follow custom. The people of this country highly honor their elders and respect the departed. The host must not be interrupted at the table.

The first toast is always for those people who have gone from this world. Then followed by a toast for the aged at the table, for ill relatives, for guests, and so on. This ritual is repeated daily in every family.

The people of this country love life and know how to live. A topic discussed in some republics to this day is whether it is possible to make money legally and if so, is being wealthy worth it. The Georgians always strive to live richly and do all they can to attain it. They always find time to work, not only for the government, but also for themselves. In the past, this was not always done legally due to the regulations.

In Georgia there were always many tourists and many Georgians rented out their homes during vacation season from May to October. Sometimes they even offered their services in the kitchen. There was always a chronic shortage of hotel rooms, especially in vacation spots, so this became an important way to earn extra money.

Some grew citrus fruit and trucked it out of the Georgian republic. Some followed Western fashions and in conjunction with government decrees produced fashionable clothes, thus earning an extra income. Many engaged in resale of domestic or imported products, which at that time was a serious criminal offense.

Georgians were ambitious for a better life and it can be said, much better prepared for the market economy than others. It's sad to see what has happened to the republic and it's people since the early 1990's.

In addition to Georgians, the Abkhazians, Adzhars, Ossetses, Russians, Armenians, Azerbaidjanis and people of other nationalities lived there for centuries. In ancient times some of them were independent countries. Outwardly it seemed they could live in peace and cooperation. With the dissolution of USSR, however, nationalism began to appear in the crudest of ways. For years a war has raged between Georgians and Abkhazians. The latter thirsted for independence. The war was bloody and continues to this day. Military maneuvers eradicated towns and villages. As a friend of mine says, the color black is more predominate in the country now.

According to tradition the period of mourning for the dead lasts for weeks, sometimes months. This dictates that women wear black. Often before the period of mourning has ended, someone else in the family dies. Sometimes women are in mourning for years. Thus is the tradition. This hard obligation of mourning falls on the shoulders of women, since for a male Georgian nothing is proscribed in this time. He can enjoy life; he can go to sporting events, theaters, restaurants, meet friends and so on. Now the war causes so many casualties that one can tell the tragedy of the people from the dress. And there is no end in sight. Occasionally there are truces, but then the war begins anew, and there are more women in black.

Nationalism is the cause of some almost unthinkable circumstances.

In Georgia there are hundreds of springs with unique healing waters. The curative powers of water at Tshaltubo are known throughout the world. Thanks to this water, many spas, modern buildings, restaurants, sports complexes, and theaters were built here. The residents of the city and nearby towns found well-paid jobs and enjoyed a high standard of living.

During the period of these nationalist wars, someone got the wild idea that it was high time to stop curing non-Georgian vacationers. Others took a more radical step and sealed the source of the spring. In an instant the city lost Russian, Armenian, Latvian and patients of many other nationalities. The city lost jobs and real hardship began. When sanity returned, it was too late. It was not easy to attract the vacationers back there. Even Nature revolted against these "wise" decisions. When the sources of the springs were unsealed, there was no water left. When the natural flow was blocked off, the stream carved itself a new path and flowed off in another direction. Sad, but true.

Georgia! A country of poets and philosophers, a country of energetic entrepreneurial people, a country of generous earth and delightful climate, a country of countless spas and tourism! I believe that soon things will improve and Georgian people will take their rightful place in the family of the peoples of the world.

Chapter 10

GORBACHEV AND THE NEW NOBILITY

The House of Unions is one of the best known buildings in Moscow. Built in the year 1780 as a mansion for a Prince, it was soon reconstructed as the Noble's Club. The main place of interest is the Hall of Columns which houses twenty-eight elegantly made columns perfectly blended into the architecture of the building. These columns make the hall of the former mansion the most refined and elegant ballroom in all of Russia. The last royal ball, at which the Czar of Russia presided, was held in 1912 and was dedicated to the one-hundred year anniversary of Russia's defeat of Napoleon.

During Soviet times, the House of Unions was a place for Communist Party Congresses, international meetings, musical competitions and concerts. In 1924 Lenin's body was displayed in the Hall for several days of public mourning. Since then the bodies of many political leaders have been shown in the Hall, including Stalin, Khrushev, and Brezhnev.

In the fall of 1990, I participated in President Gorbachev's first meeting with representatives of the Union of Entrepreneurs at the Hall of Columns. These newly created entrepreneurs eagerly sought such a meeting for more than two years. Gorbachev seemed to find many excuses to avoid meetings with this rising social group, although the real reasons were obvious to everyone.

While it may have looked like he was trying to make significant changes, in actuality he tried only to improve the existing social system and to make socialism look "more human" —a popular slogan of those years. Communicating publicly with these businessmen would have demonstrated to all that President Gorbachev shared the entrepreneurial goals of this group and that he was ready for revolutionary economic changes. It was obvious to all that he was not really ready to take such a dramatic step.

On the other hand, ignoring significant changes was also not possible. His policy of waiting had already brought him to political isolation by that time.

In 1988 the long-standing conflict between Armenia and Azerbijan erupted into bloody warfare, known as the Karabakh Conflict. The Armenians were struggling for the right of their people, who lived in part of Azerbijan, to be independent and self-determining. Their real objective was a free state within Azerbijan controlled and governed by Armenian ethnic people. Azerbijan tried to maintain the integrity of their republic by any means and was unwilling to compromise in any way.

During several months of the conflict, hundreds of people were killed, mostly Armenians. In the beginning, President Gorbachev was unable or unwilling to make any decisions to help bring an end to the killing. Many politicians of middle and high rank tried to solve the conflict. Finally, Gorbachev took some steps but it was already to late! They did not take him seriously. A short time before, the word of even a mid-level party leader or government official was accepted as the word of law. Now there was total lack of respect and credibility for even the President of the entire Soviet Union.

This rejection began to be seen as Gorbachev's weakness. It became obvious to everyone that he lacked a strong will which was necessary for the country's leader to demonstrate at this crucial time. Many other republics had been covertly trying to separate themselves from Moscow's governance. At first they used hidden tactics for economic independence. After the Karabakh Conflict these republics became open in their rebellion against the political control of a strong central government. The Karabakh Conflict had become a turning point for Gorbachev's leadership. He was tested and he failed.

Gorbachev widely publicized his concept of *Glastnost*, a doctrine of personal freedom. This emphasis was critical to the people of the Soviet Union and became equally important to the future of the entire world. Gorbachev promulgated this policy of personal freedom in a country which had been dedicated to totalitarian rule for many generations. Because he created a climate of change for personal freedoms in such a resistive society, in this respect history will forever hold President Gorbachev in high regard.

On April 29, 1986, something happened that changed the future for Gorbachev and the USSR forever.

In Chernobyl, a small industrial town near Kiev in Ukraine, there was an explosion at a nuclear power plant. The whole world was anxious about the dire consequences of this accident and waited to see what steps the Soviet government would follow to minimize risk to its citizens, neighbors, and the whole world. However, the Soviet people did not know anything about Chernobyl for several days.

May 1 (May Day) was an official day of celebration. People throughout the Soviet Union traditionally walk in the parks and forest to mark the day with great joy. In spite of the catastrophe, Gorbachev decided not to cancel the celebrations on May 1 in the cities and villages close to Chernobyl. Not knowing the real situation, millions of people wandered into local forests and parks in these terrible days only to learn later that they had recieved excessive amounts of radiation. The health of millions was put at great risk and thousands died.

This happened because President Gorbachev decided not to tell the truth and people close to him revealed how much he regretted his decision. His face became older in just a matter of days. He appeared confused and disorientated as he reviewed Moscow's May Day parade. These were days of dramatic change for Gorbachev.

He was treated differently by everyone. Publicity treated Gorbachev well in those cases when he criticized his predecessors with no fear of them because they were no longer alive. He had long preached the "religion" of *Glasnost*, or the right to freely express oneslf. Now that it was no longer expedient for him, he did not act as he preached. He talked about it for everyone else but did not follow it himself. The cornerstone of Gorbachev's reform was taken away by Gorbachev himself.

Gorbachev wanted positive change in the economy, but his economic reforms did not work. The Soviet economy had been disintegrating for many years. The small steps of reform proposed by Gorbachev were unable even to begin to change the situation. Things were getting worse each day. Clothes, food, and gasoline were lacking throughout the country. Even in Moscow there were huge lines of people waiting for hours to get a loaf of bread.

Instead, Gorbachev gave regular TV reports which glowingly told how successful the country had been in finishing a particular step of his reform and how additional economic improvements would be seen even the very next day. People looked in surprise at each other because they could see the failure of these reforms every day.

The most popular saying of those days was "When you listen to Gorbachev, shut the doors and windows in order not to see the striking difference between what the President is saying and the reality of life." Many people wondered if he knew the real situation in the country or whether he was just another insincere leader communicating poorly with his people. This opinion reflected negatively on Gorbachev's leadership.

In announcing bold new reforms in a country where changes came slowly, Gorbachev risked the displeasure of his comrades in the Communist Party. Still, he forged ahead, knowing that he would never be forgiven by roughly twenty million fellow comrades. In just one day he proposed sweeping changes, and he lost the support of the party members.

Because of a lack of resources he began to cut military spending. That was enough to lose support of this powerful faction. He made public unlawful financial activities of some military leaders, especially those who served in East Germany. This caused the rift between Gorbachev and the military to widen.

Ordinary working people did not really understand the reform policies of the President. His western-like claims of the priority of human values over the interests of the country and its collective citizens were unsettling to people.

The only thing that the people saw around him or her was a "special" kind of democracy that was corrupt, anarchistic, and filled with civil strife.

Nor did Gorbachev find understanding and support among the intelligentsia. Actually, they were more in opposition than anyone else. It was the first time in history that a leader of Russia actually tried to turn the political establishment towards democratic reforms. The "intelligentsia," who usually espoused movement to more liberal reforms, now held tight onto traditional politics to protect their place in the emerging society. Many of them abandoned their traditional role in society as teachers and educators and lined up with the business and leadership structures of the country. This was not a matter of ideals, rather it was a chance to solidify their individual opportunity for power, land, and position in the new economy of Russia.

Gorbachev's attempts to bring something new to the development of Soviet society seemed too revolutionary for many people. For others it seemed insufficient. Gorbachev, in only three years, lost the support of the most significant power groups within the country. More and more he isolated himself and was seen as a weak leader. At this same time, the western governments and media portrayed him as a strong leader succeeding in democratic reforms in the USSR.

Among the debris, there emerged a new social class; the entrepreneurs. In the beginning this class had supported Gorbachev's new policy. This was the basis of their very existence, but Gorbachev did not share their wishes. In 1990 in the Hall of Columns Gorbachev looked for support from those who benefited most of all from his new politics, from those who became very rich in just a few days as if by magic. Some of them became incredibly rich. Ten people from the former USSR became listed as the top 100 of the richest people in the world according to *Forbes* magazine.

Where did these first "soviet" capitalists come from? Prior to 1987 all businesses were part of the Soviet collective system. After 1987, Gorbachev opened the way to create some private businesses, known as "cooperatives." These new businesses were established in the trading, agricultural, manufacturing, and construction industries. It was expected that these operations would increase production of necessary goods, reduce costs, and change the economy as a whole. However, this was done without the gradual changes that were so essential for the transition to capitalism and away from the basic laws that governed the socialistic economy.

As is often the case in the USSR, everything happened "backwards."

After two years it was evident that there were no changes in the overall economy, but only the development of a system of exclusive ownership by a new, very small minority of businessmen. Less than 3% of total goods and services were produced by these "new" businesses. Only 13% of them were formed independently. The remaining 87% of these private enterprises were formed by other entrepreneurs and the leaders of larger centralized companies for their own financial interests. These smaller businesses were subsidized by free raw materials and free access to the production equipment of the parent. As the large companies gave support to their smaller offspring enterprises, they were able to dramatically reduce their cost, much to the personal financial interest of the leaders of the large companies and some government representatives.

Additionally, the legal and economic climate allowed entrepreneurs and highly placed corporate people to convert corporate assets to personal wealth. Within this cooperative environment many became wealthy overnight. This was the first accumulation of capital by individuals in the USSR.

In this former socialistic country they were the first true capitalists, the first millionaires and even the first billionaires. Then these people took unlimited advantage in the process of privatization of State property.

Fifteen years have gone by and the struggle for private ownership of former government property has not abated. Some entrepreneurs have risen to new heights; some have fallen. Under President Putin, there is again a trend to nationalize private property. Currently however, this is focused only on the most wealthy. For example, in 2004 the wealth of Russia's richest and most successful businessman, Micheal Hodarkhovskiy, was taken over by the the state and he was sentenced to nine years in prison. The basis for financial success for those so "lucky" to succeed, including many government officials, was created during the Gorbachev period of so-called "cooperative movement."

In 1990 these so-called "New Russians" met in the most prestigious building in the country, the Hall of Columns. There were about 500 people from all over the Soviet Union. They controlled the greatest share of wealth in the entire country. They were rich, independent, and in control. They no longer needed anything from Gorbachev.

In his first official meeting with these new owners, Gorbachev was so unprepared that many in attendance started to lose patience with him. Suddenly, there were shouts from the audience: "Time, Time." The President of the country was being told, in no uncertain terms, to leave the podium.

Gorbachev spent some time trying to turn this obvious defeat into a joke of some sort.

I was in the very front of that Hall and had the chance to view the smallest details of that duel. Gorbachev lost again. The audience's chant of "Time, Time" had another symbolic meaning: "Your time as a political leader, Mr. President, is over." Gorbachev lost his last opportunity for political support. Even these entrepreneurs and businessmen that he had created withdrew from him. He was in total isolation. The President now represented only himself, not any of his country's people.

One year later he experienced something extraordinary. He became the President of a country, the Soviet Union, that did not exist. There was now Russia and the fourteen Newly Independent States (NIS). Did Gorbachev understand what was really going on? Probably not. If he had understood, he would not have tried again in 1996 to revive himself as a political leader. In 1996, as in 1990, he was supported by only one per cent of the population. After a crushing defeat in 1996, he finally understood that his time was indeed over and his dream of political revenge was impossible.

And what about the "New Russians?" They were the new "nobility" of the country. They continued to grow more successful. They proceeded to build their own palaces, many as luxurious and lavish as the Hall of Columns where only a few years before they had first met as a legal social group. These people prospered while the economy around them stagnated. For the most part the privatized businesses only produced half as many products as they did before privatization.

Historically in a free market, following the accumulation of the capital, there has been a period of reinvestment and economic improvement.

In Russia and the NIS, this did not happen initially. While there has been some improvement, this new wealth was used by the entrepreneurs to invest in a variety of opportunities outside of Russia and the NIS. The question to be asked is when and how can this continuing accumulation of wealth be effectively put to use internally to aid in the expansion of these countries' economies.

These "New Russians," as a part of a corporate-criminal system, made small enterprises almost totally dependent on them. Controlling most national resources, they created different kinds of extortion for farmers, factory owners, restaurants, and others and generally put small business in a critically difficult position. Even today the small business owner or the farmer in reality, is more like hired help rather than real owners of their own business. Nothing like this has happened in the history of business, except when a small group of self-interested business and government people are in control of the economy.

Observing the economic success of the United States and Western Europe, Russia, and the NIS attempted to generally follow their economic model. By attempting to duplicate today's Western economic system, Russia and the NIS missed the fact that the economy can only function properly when a sound manufacturing base is in place. While this was finally understood by many, in practice little was been done to address this fundamental axiom. By indices of economic development and competitiveness, for example, Russia still holds merely 64th place of the eighty most developed countries of the world. Because of this millions of people living in the NIS feel they are not able, irrespective of their age, education, or experience, to be productive for their families and their country. Only 25% of the population has a better life now then at the beginning of the 1990s. The remaining 75% live in significantly worse conditions with tens of millions of people below the poverty level.

The "New Russians" created a unique economy in their countries. It is hard to tell whether the present economic system or an economic system controlled by a minority has the priority. It remains unclear what part of the new economy follows the principles of capitalism and what part follows the centralized system. Is the prevalent force the rule of law or the self-interested minority seeking their own wealth at the expense of everyone else? Today's economy looks something like a form of capitalism, but it is not really capitalism yet. The way to the free market is long and difficult.

Chapter 11

THE DARK SIDE OF A REVOLUTIONARY TIME

Not many people have the opportunity to see the disintegration of a huge empire within a three to four year period.

On one hand, I am fortunate that I was a mature, experienced observer of the change from socialism to capitalism first hand. I was able to understand with both my mind and my heart the events which were taking place as well as their influence on the fate of the people of many countries and on the whole world as well.

On the other hand, during this revolutionary time, I, like millions of others, lost everything that I had managed to amass through thirty-eight years of hard work. I lost my savings (in 1992 inflation was 3000%), my home and everything in it, my job, and my friends. For the sake of our lives and for the future of the children, at the age of fifty-seven I decided to emigrate to the United States with my family.

The more significant the changes taking place in society, the more interesting it is for the historian and the more difficult it is for those who are trying to live through it. Thousands of books, articles, and analyses have been written about Michel Gorbachev, his work, and consequences of his actions.

Nevertheless, some aspects of life during that period went almost unnoticed. I, for one, was profoundly effected by these changes, as were many people that I had known for decades. They changed in appearance and behavior and not always for the better.

Mark Twain noticed that humanity, like the moon, has two sides: the light and the dark. Under normal conditions it is not so simple to see the true face of a people. But during extreme revolutionary conditions, hour by hour, bit by bit, people are shown to be what they really are.

Yesterday my colleague and neighbor was a good friend with a harmonious family. He was a man who understood the value of love and the importance of mutual understanding in a family. But today, fighting for the purity of the nation, he insists on the breakup of marriages between people of different nationalities. As for such little "details" as love, children, and decades of life lived together, he simply avoids discussion.

Yesterday, he was a liberal to the marrow of his bones and the first to support the impractical idea of the eradication of national differences and the integration of an indivisible community of "Soviet People." But today he is working on the New Laws Project, which will divide the people of the republic into different categories by nationality; giving them different rights ranging from full privileges to almost no rights at all.

Yesterday he stood in the first row of fighters for peace and order in the country, a champion for strong government. Now he supports a war: war between Armenians and the Azerbaijanis, between the Uzbekistans and the Kyrgyz, between the Moldavians and the Ukrainians, between the Russians and the Chechens. At times prolonged and bloody wars totally decimated cities and villages. The winner, having either forgotten or not realized that it is already the end of the 20th century, is still bonding people into slavery.

Yesterday, he admired the heroic deeds of the World War II veterans and wrote songs and poems in their honor. Today, he scorns and detests them. He acts as if these modest and courageous people went to their death or lost their mothers, children, brothers and sisters because they chose to. During the Gorbachev era everyone's hindsight became so keen that they suddenly forgot that under the most extreme form of Stalinist authoritarian government, people were not only unable to influence the politics of the state but were afraid even to voice their own opinion at home. So why should we cast blame on these same simple persons, who were just as distant from politics then, as today's critics are from ethics?

Yesterday, he was an advocate of political pluralism and passionately defended the right of different parties to participate in the political life of the country. Today he organizes a group of demonstrators who occupy the entranceway to the parliament building. Before the very eyes of the police they brutally beat an opposition party member to the point where, afraid for his life, he forever loses interest in taking part in political activities.

Yesterday, you were a respected doctor, teacher, professor, or engineer. Your patient, student, or colleague paid you every possible sign of respect. Now they don't even say hello; you get a cold stare instead, as if you are responsible for everything that is wrong with the world. This is simply because you are not a member of the group accepted as "native nationality." Everything else is forgotten, including those truly courageous, extraordinary people who first gave voice to freedom of speech and freedom of conscience. These people were talking about freedom and market economics as much as twenty-five years before the Perestroika and paid for it with humiliation, loss of work, the means to subsist, and even sentenced to jail.

Yesterday he was an atheist. Moreover, he was a professor of Marxist philosophy and gave lectures about atheism at the university. Today he is not only in the first row of those who are attending church or synagogue, he is the moving force behind the church or synagogue organization or has even become a minister or rabbi.

Yesterday he hid his own social background from everyone and prospered in life. No one knew, nor was supposed to know, that he came from nobility, or a merchant family or that his father was a priest or rabbi. Today he is forming the New Nobility Society or the Cossack Society, or some other group that was previously forbidden and has put himself in a new wave of people building second careers, to fare even better than they did in the previous social order.

Yesterday he was an expert on the law, firmly standing guard to ensure its observance. Today he lives in Moscow as public prosecutor. Having forgotten about his professional functions and duties at a session of a court of law, he suddenly denies the charges. By doing this he protects the editor of a fascist oriented newspaper, which was acknowledged to be guilty of activities aimed at inciting nationalistic and religious animosity. It is truly a unique case in the annals of world jurisprudence when a public prosecutor protects the guilty.

Russians in the national republics occupy key positions. A Russian serves as the Deputy Secretary of the Communist Party for the republic. He implements Moscow policy which, in effect, controls all life and activity in the region. Also a Russian was the Chief of the KGB, the Commander in Chief of the armed forces, stationed in a territory of the republic, the Assistant Secretary of State and so forth. Together with representatives of other nationalities, these Russians worked in different positions in industry, agriculture, science, art, construction, and transportation.

These positions were different, but irrespective of that, they all were proud of the nationality to which they belonged. They conducted themselves independently and looked down on people of different nationalities. The growing zeal and aspirations of minority group members to produce higher quality work than that of others, and their cautions against speaking out was surprising to Russians. It was as though minority group members simply took pride in their work which they had acquired with such great difficulty, and were afraid lest if they spoke out they should be deprived of it. However, all this was just yesterday.

Today the republics have become independent governments, and overnight the Russians have become second or even third class citizens. Because of political instability and economic difficulties within Russia itself, and also because of the mutual resentment which has built up over long decades between the central government and the national territories, Moscow is no longer able to influence the fate of these people.

The Russian, who just yesterday was so proud, now grovels before those whom, only days before, he blamed for an absence of character. He, who only yesterday was brave and independent in his utterances, today has become quite careful of his words, unsure of his actions, and on the whole, a confused person. Today he is in the minority, whereas before he was so comfortable as part of the majority.

Moreover, many Russians, Ukrainians, Azerbaijanis, etc., having forgotten about their nationalistic pride, tried to find any possible way via any distant Jewish or German relative in their pedigree to get to permanent domicile in Israel, the United States, or Germany.

People change before our very eyes. At times their actions border on the comically grotesque. For instance in the span of mere days one scholar wrote a treatise on how to bring about transformation from socialism to capitalism within a time frame of one and a half years. It was handled as if the question was about a technical problem in which every variable could be calculated and foreseen in advance rather than a dialogue about the highly complex socio-economic metamorphosis of a multinational government.

In another region a poet decided to register her marriage with an eminent statesman who lived 400 years ago! No one was particularly surprised by that. The true faces of the whole organizations were exposed. The Moldavian Writers Union and the Women's Organization of the Republic stated their platform on the national question succinctly: Russians should stay on the other side of the Dnister River (along which runs the border between Moldova and Ukraine), and Jews should be drowned in it.

With sadness and anxiety, I, along with a thousand others, observed all of these changes. I often discussed the situation with close friends and others, especially those who belonged to the small—read inferior—nationalities. Among them were an Armenian, Arcadiy Shakildyan (a scholar), a Greek, Evgeny Pampasx (the chief designer of a pump factory), a Jew, Abraham Golfer (the Department Head of the Ministry of Local Industry), Tatar Rafic Raice (service industry),and others.

Michel Gorbachov's glasnost was universally hailed because at last it gave the people of the biggest country in the world the chance to express their views openly and without fear. This was done to promote the progress of social development. However freedom without justice, responsibility, kindness and intelligence has become a terrible and malicious creature.

For a hundred years the people of this country were deprived of freedom and rights, especially during the Stalinist period. Unfortunately, the shortcomings of democracy reduced the happiness of people and slowed the progress of the economy. Now after literally just months of rejoicing, many began to realize that democracy without limits and its "abundance" leads society to instability and destruction. It is strange, but in a country where people only had a just little taste of freedom, they began to understand that even long-awaited democracy is useful only in carefully prescribed doses.

Perestroika and subsequent economic reforms were developed in order to give the emerging newly independant states and expanded regions the ability to decide when and how to make the practical decisions needed to improve the stagnant economy and to raise the standard of living. In practice, however, for many months or even a few years, the new leaders continued a political game with the masses in street demonstrations, ignoring the situation with manufacturing. In a country with a shortage of absolutely everything from bread to bicycles and tractors, many years after the collapse of the former USSR, people lived with a focus on change. They were thinking only about trade and not how to make goods.

The decision of new leaders to destroy in one day the economic connections which had been in place for decades between the former republics completely paralyzed production. The unemployment rate in some republics reached astronomic proportions, 36-50% of the workforce. The economic interdependence of these regions was already quite significant. As late as the early 90's even a large republic such as Ukraine was able to supply only 20% of the total resources needed for production. For the other 80% of needed energy resources, raw materials, assembled and unassembled parts, it had to depend of other republics. It will take years to understand how destructive and ruinous this decision was for the economy. In principle the regions are once again returning to their former partners to regain industrial connections.

All of this pales in comparison, however, with how human nature has been transformed in the battle over the redistribution of property for private use. Many recognize the key factors: fraud, thievery, bribery, treachery, abduction, and murder. These were everyday occurrences in every village, town, and city at that time.

At the same time in each collective group of people there were many noble, honest, and truly intelligent individuals who had to endure the difficulties and adversities of unsuccessful economic experiments during the transitional period.

Our neighbor, Tamara Michailovna, a Russian, invited my family to her house before our departure because it was dangerous for people emigrating to the USA and Israel to stay home alone, due to the possibilities of being beaten or killed, especially at night. Another woman named Tamara Greku, a Moldavian by nationality, without any thoughts of payment agreed to look after the graves of my father and my wife's parents for several years. A Bulgarian named Evgeny Khrishchev, who was a department head at a university and president of the academic council there, asked me to serve as a member of a doctoral defense committee in economics. I noted that I might already be living in another country on the day of the defense. But professor Khrishchev insisted, stating that my opinion as a specialist would be important for the dissertation committee. If it happened that my departure would interfere with the process, then the faculty advisor on the committee would present my opinion and comments. That is what happened.

On December 14, 1992, I came to America. While in Rochester, New York, on December 27, mastering my very first words in English, I still "served" as a member of that dissertation committee in Chisinau (Moldova). To this day from among numerous thesis abstracts, I have kept a copy of that work as evidence of a normal, productive relationship with the scientific community.

On the day of my departure a few of my acquaintances in Moscow came to the International Airport to say good-bye and to give me a few copies of a newspaper in which an article about me and my work as a scholar and businessman was published. The newspaper, *Business World* (December 8, 1992), had prepared this article for publication many months ago, but it was released only four days prior.

I will not soon forget this moment. While I was saying farewell to several business colleagues, one gave me a bottle of champagne and told me to save it for December 31st so that I could drink to the health and well-being of my family in America on New Years Eve of 1993. I could go on giving examples of the wonderful relationship between me and people of the most varied nationalities and professions during that difficult period of my life. The negative effects on people were far greater and more visible in a rapidly changing society. They took risks just being nice to me.

Revolutions take place because it is impossible to continue to live as in the past. Therefore, during such a period changes in consciousness, behavior, and in interactions with others are natural. The involvement of new people in the administration of government is understandable. Nevertheless, the new society is in need of new people who not only are ready to occupy key positions but who also will take responsibility for making very complicated decisions. In short, without proper changes taking place within the individual, no other type of change in society is possible.

In the early 90s, the world became aware of the tragic events related to the collapse of Yugoslavia. The collapse was bought about due to the clash of the ethnic cultures and religous differences (orthodoxy, caltholicism and islam) of the people. Before this, I had the opportunity to travel there and see the unusual natural beauty of its mountains, rivers, seas and forests. I saw the architecture of her cities and villages with my own eyes and personally experienced the hospitality and special culture of the people living in this land, and became convinced of the particularly high standard of living that they had at that time.

I later often thought about what could happen to the people of that country if hundreds of thousands of them were to instantly lose the capacity to think sensibly about what is most important in life, about the boundary between good and evil. Were that to occur, they too would be drawn toward evil. Before long, evil thoughts turned into evil actions in Yugoslavia. This was a repeat of what had been experienced by many territories of the former USSR, such as Armenia, Azerbaijan, Moldova and Kirgiz.

Clearly, it is easier to critically evaluate the activities of others than to make the right decisions oneself during a complex transitional period. I was a scientific adviser during the first phase of Perestroika (1987-92) and understood the difficulties.

Three limiting factors partially explain why, in a country with vast natural resources and a multitude of talented people, the transition to democracy and a free market would turn out to be so painful that to this day it has remained unsuccessful in many parts of the former USSR.

First, the newness of the problems and complete lack of experience in resolving them. Never before had a revolutionary transformation taken place without some mistakes and backtracking. However, the transition from a planned economy to a free market was taking place for the first time in the history of mankind, therefore the difficulty of this path was unique.

This did not take place in the ideological, organizational, or financial spheres. The country was poorly prepared for these types of radical changes.

One group of reformers underestimated the importance of such preliminary work. Another group resigned themselves to the belief that during a revolutionary period it is easier to follow in the wave of spontaneous events than to control them. A third group consciously tried to pay no heed to all of this.

Many were surprised at how easy it was for responsible people to adapt to the impending changes. One person imagined that it would be sufficient to change three or four people in the party leadership and that all the problems there would be resolved. Another never doubted that the key to the success was to improve the representation of a certain nation in key economic positions. A third, in answer to a question, about how he saw the future of Perestroika, said that he was an optimist and that he already could see the "light at the end of the tunnel."

Actually, as a highly intelligent man with a good

understanding of the situation, he was thinking something quite different.

Even Michel Gorbachev every two to three months reported on the successful completion of one stage of Perestroika and the transition to the next stage. The economy was actually getting worse each day. If asked whether real reforms were taking place in the economy at that time, people would sadly answer in the affirmative—if life were treated abstractly and judged the changes only by what was seen on television or in newspaper articles.

At the same time as the transition from a planned economy to a capitalist system of economics, another complex problem was in the process of being resolved. The people in the national republics were trying to get independence from Russia. In the majority of cases it was their striving for independence and not the transition to the market economy which had primary importance.

Finally, given the complexity of the problems, they should have been resolved by the most knowledgeable and talented people available, who had enough courage and know-how to get things moving in the right direction.

Unfortunately, this did not occur. In the republics the preeminent role was played by the writers—representatives of the creative intelligentsia—who often were not practical scholars. As it turned out, those who having quickly reorganized the bureaucracy of the former official state machinery turned out to be ambitious climbers who were more interested in their personal fortunes than in the fate of the country's people. In short, there was no professionalism in the strategies used to make these changes. One cannot expect good to come of such situations.

The French philosopher Charles Montesquieu, who lived

and worked in the 17th and 18th centuries, writing of similar situations, said, "Scholars are wonderful people, and the peasants are wonderful people, but the problems of society arise because they are each only half-educated."

Chapter 12

Unfinished Home

For most of the 20th century millions of people in the Soviet Union worked hard, but were unable to make their lives any easier. Why was their hard work not rewarded? By describing the experiences of my family, I can explain the struggles of many others.

I have a big family. My paternal grandfather had six sons and three daughters. My maternal grandfathers had five sons and seven daughters. Each of them had at least three children. Consequently, I have an impressively large number of cousins. They had a wide range of occupations; from agriculture to manufacturing, construction trade, and other industries. They worked in many different places—Ukraine, Moldova, Byelorussia, Uzbekhistan, Kazakhstan, and Russia, including Siberia and the North Pole. The lives of each family member was different depending on their generation, their natural environment, and personal aspirations.

Unfinished House

My mother's father, Isaac, lived in the village of Dzygovka, which is ten miles from my town of Yampol. He was a rather prosperous farmer with his own piece of land and some agricultural equipment, two cows, and three horses. Isaac worked hard and taught his children from their early years to do the same. Farming was hard work; nobody thought about studying.

Isaac was a very handy man. He was a carpenter, a painter, and a builder. It had been his life's dream to build a five room house for his family of eight people. He managed to build the outside walls as well as a roof and to finish three rooms. He did not finish the other two rooms or the other buildings that he had intended to build because he was afraid.

It was the 1920's, the period of the collectivization of agriculture, a period when individually owned properties were stolen by the government and the farms were destroyed in the USSR. This government action negatively impacted agricultural production for the next sixty years in the Soviet Union.

In order to avoid deportation to Siberia in 1929, Isaac voluntarily gave his property to the collective farm, "Arbait." Like other collective farmers he worked from early morning until late at night. His payment was grain rather than money. The annual crop production varied. In a good year he received more, but in a bad year he received no more than was necessary to keep his family from starving to death.

Collective farms operated with three major objectives. The first priority was to provide government warehouses with agricultural output; the second was to pay off government debt; and the third was to provide ordinary workers with remuneration. My grandfather was a physically strong man. He was not afraid of work. Deep inside, however, he regretted losing his property. It was all that he had to show for his work. The loss somehow influenced his personality. Over all he was most profoundly upset by the position of the peasants as being little more than slaves.

Before Nikita Khrushchev's changes in agricultural strategy in the mid 1950's, the peasants were actually "stuck to the soil," having no right to leave it. Over three decades (1929–1958), the collective farmers were not given identification documents or passports. During those times people were not allowed to move without this document. Exceptions were allowed on an individual basis, provided there was a serious reason that met the collective farm leaders' approval. This process made it nearly impossible to move to a town or city, and thus it was nearly impossible for anyone to change his trade.

My grandfather worked in a collective farm up to the time the Germans conquered the Ukraine in 1941. Later after surviving the fascists' concentration camp, he returned to his home only to discover that it had been robbed by members of the local population. He lived there for four more years and died in his still unfinished house.

A Small Businessman

My other grandfather, Shiy, worked in the fruit business. He dried plums. He also bought and sold other kinds of fruit. Unlike Isaac, he did not have his own plot of land or gardens. During the best of times he owned only three or four pieces of drying apparatus, yet he was proud to have them. In order to feed his family of twelve (his wife, nine children and a blind sister), he had to put his sons to work around the time they turned twelve years old. Revolutions, wars, pogroms, and massacres continually gave Shiy more challenges.

Three times—in 1905, 1918, and 1921—Shiy was forced to start his small business from scratch. Consequently, his family never lived a rich life, but they did not starve either. Although they did not own much, what they did own had special meaning to them.

Shiy's business was most successful during the period of Lenin's New Economic Policy in the beginning of 1920's. In 1917 the property of the richest segment of the population was taken over by the State. In 1921 Lenin, the first leader of the first socialist state, observed the results of the socialist economic methods of management and administration. Within three years he concluded that the system was not working as he had envisioned it.

Major differences of opinion about this were found within the Communist leadership. Lenin forced modifications to the system in order to motivate productivity.

From 1918 to 1921 the government would take 90 % of all goods produced. According to the New Policy small farmers and businessmen were obligated to pay fixed taxes in cash or in kind to the government. With this new freedom and initiative, additional goods produced were the individual's property. Step by step, thanks to the great motivation of the average person, the economy became more productive. The life of an ordinary citizen improved significantly. Some became wealthy.

At the end of the 1920's after Lenin's death, Stalin canceled Lenin's directions. For the second time the government forcibly nationalized the private property of the "new rich." These changes applied to everyone, even to such small businessmen as my grandfather. Those who tried to raise objections against this policy were repressed. Shiy adhered to the new government policy and gave up his drying business. He gave his equipment to the collective farm. For almost five years, Shiy continued to work with his own equipment but only as an employee. Later he lost his job, but by that time his sons were employed elsewhere and were able to help him and his daughters.

Altogether, Shiy worked for fifty-five years. During those years he was only able to buy a small two room apartment for his family. The apartment was sparsely furnished with beds made of metal, three to four stools, a table and an ancient dresser. More important than material possessions Shiy cared about his reputation and the reputation of his family. He was well known and respected in his town. Shiy was a great family man and brought up his sons to be a good family men as well, and he loved his grandchildren.

I can still remember well that time when I was only five years old and visited him in his home. It was a special, warm atmosphere. I remember the delicious food. We had salad made of radishes, boiled buckwheat, corn flour dishes, and potatoes with herring. Back then it was common for families, grandparents, children and grandchildren to get together on weekends and eat such meals together. Shiy perished in a concentration camp in 1942.

Trading a Home for a Dozen Eggs

My father, Samuel, was most dear to me. He deserves to have his own memoir specially dedicated to him. However, I am not able to do this since my father was never willing to share much of his past. He was a man of action rather than words. Furthermore, he was not expressive. Having two mothers, I had three grandmothers and three grandfathers. All but two of them, Isaac and Shiy, died before I was able to learn much about them.

Although I wish I could have learned more details of my father's life, I only know a few. He started working when he was twelve years old. When he was twenty-two, he married the most beautiful girl in the town. Many people who knew my parents at that time frequently told me they were a beautiful couple. Their love was special. I was born a year after they were married. Eight months later my mother, Cecilia, died. When I was in my thirties, I was given two pictures by cousin Mara to remember my mother. I have carefully guarded these pictures, since the war took away everything, including all of the pictures of my family.

After my mother's sudden death many people, especially our extended family, tried to help my father. But he took the most care of me. By that time two of my grandmothers had already died. The third was sick and often needed care. The men were busy providing for their own families.

When I was a baby, my father had a busy schedule. He worked ten hour days for a regional industrial enterprise as a furrier. During his two-hour lunch break, relieved my grandmother of her responsibilities. Back then he did not have the conveniences of today like running water, diapers, baby formula, etc. Neither did he have sufficient supplies of basics such as soap and blankets. Despite continual challenges he never complained. He just did what he had to do.

A year and a half after my mother's death, my father married for the second time. His new wife, Betty, was six years younger. Despite all of life's difficulties, they lived happily in love for fifty-five years.

In 1939, when I was three years old, my father was drafted into the army to support his country in the Soviet-Finnish War. In June 1941 on the third day after the Germans invaded the USSR, my father rejoined the army. It was the most frightening war in the history of humanity. Although I was only five years old, I still remember that day as clearly as if it happened yesterday.

The men, young and old, in good health or not, Ukrainians, Russians, Jews, and Poles, all found seats in trucks. That day for the last time we saw my father and four of his five brothers together. The fifth brother lived in another town. I was unable to understand anything clearly, but somehow I was able to sense the misfortune.

Not bothered by the crying, screaming, and hysterics of the women and elderly around me, I can still remember looking at my father until the truck disappeared around the corner. There was only one thought in my little head at that time. "My father is leaving me." Whether he chose to leave or whether he was forced to did not matter at that time. I felt deprived of the only thing in my life that seemed to matter.

After walking thousands of miles and after years of fighting with the enemy, my father was dismissed from the war near Budapest, Hungary in October 1945.

Only my father and one of his five brothers came back home alive. The other four had perished. The day after he returned home, my father started working again. He worked at the same regional industrial enterprise where he worked before the war and in the same capacity. His life was not easy. He feared for his earnings. Similar to thousands of other people from his generation, my father worked many seven day weeks. He never experienced vacations. His dream to rest by the sea was never fulfilled.

My father tried to save money on everything. In 1956 he bought a small house with two rooms and a kitchen. In 1980 I helped my parents purchase a home in the city of Chishinau, Moldova, where my family and I lived and worked. My father sold his house in Yampol for nine thousand rubles. We all were happy and my father was the happiest of all. He had his savings, which he thought would provide a secure retirement fund. He did not want to become dependent on his children. He saved this money in a bank account which paid him three percent interest. My father chose not to use his savings and used only the interest for spending money.

My father experienced many financial loses in his life. Like others, he was underpaid for his work. Workers like him only earned half of the wages they should have received. Also, along with millions of other employees, he was forced to buy the obligations of Government loans.

In buying these obligations, he understood that he was losing his money forever. He remembered all those monetary reforms he lived through. Is it possible to forget when overnight your savings have been devalued by 90%? That happened three times during his life.

But in 1992 as a result of the economic reform of Mr. Gaidar, the First Deputy Prime Minister in Yeltsin's first cabinet, the inflation became astronomically high. The value of money decreased by 3000% from 1987 to 1992. For the 9,000 rubles my father had saved, he could only buy a dozen eggs. In the worst horror story you could not find such an exchange—a house for

My father Samuel, myself, my younger brother Yafim, my step-mother Betty, and younger sister Lisa.

a dozen eggs. My father could not accept what had happened to his money. He was quite sick at that time, and his heart could not tolerate the loss. He died in May 1992. Like his father and his ancestors, he died in poverty. He was poor financially but rich in many other ways.

I often think of my father. I remember him as a hard worker, always worrying about his earnings. He lived for his family. He worried about me, my sister, and my younger brother whenever something wrong happened to us. I recollect the happy days of his life. Those times usually involved his children.

He loved all his grandchildren greatly, but when his great-grandchild (my sister Lisa's grandchild) was born, he was especially happy. He had much joy when my brother Yafim, the youngest child in our family, got married. That day many of our close relatives from various cities of the country gathered together. Many of them came because they wanted to see my father too. My father, the oldest in the family, was proud of his children, his nephews, and his nieces. He was proud of the achievements of all of us together and each of us individually.

Another of my special memories of my father dates back to 1969. It was the day we attended the banquet honoring the successful defense of my Doctoral dissertation. One famous scientist from the Ukraine spoke with my father. After their conversation the scientist said to the audience that it was pleasant to see someone so educated by nature, my father. It is difficult to describe how much that meant to my father and to all of us. We all knew well the difficulties of my father's childhood and why he was prevented him from getting an education. We also knew how much he valued education.

In 1987 we attended another banquet. This one honored

my new lifetime title as Doctor and Professor. While hearing all the good words being said about me, I realized that the biggest part of my success in life was due to my father. I stood up, raised my glass and asked everyone to drink to "my roots," to my parents. Many people knew my deep feelings toward my father. Everyone gave him a standing ovation. My father was surprised. He was not accustomed to such moments.

When I looked at him during those minutes, I was thinking that possibly society would soon learn to value the life and deeds of not just the talented and gifted people, but of ordinary people like my father, who were modest, hardworking and devoted to their families. Such people are in the majority in each country. In both normal and extreme situations the most is taken from these same people. I always tried to be attentive to my father. However, when he died, I reproached myself many times that I had not done much more for him.

A Real Mother: My Stepmother Betty

Many Russian traditions say, expect nothing good from a stepmother. Some people felt sorry for me, and some tried to help me. All this poisoned my childhood so much that for many years, I judged any action of my mother from one view only: a stepmother is not a real mother. I grew up self-centered. I did not let anyone get close to me. Several years later I saw for myself how nicely my stepmother was raising my younger sister and brother. I realized that although she was strict and demanding, she was fair.

My mother was attentive to everything that went on in our family. She taught us to keep everything in order. She taught us to be responsible for what we did. A person with a strong character and a sharp mind, she saved our family from many extremely difficult life situations during World War II and after the War. She loved me the same as the children to whom she gave life. Hence I had two mothers. One was my biological mother whom I can not remember. The other was the mother who raised me and to whom I owe so much.

When I was an adult, I tried to show my gratitude and to give my attention in any possible way to that hardworking and most noble woman. But is it possible for children to be so kind and good to parents that they can ever completely pay for what their parents did for them?

The Fallen Saviors

In 1964, I married Valentine. The university building where my classes took place was one block from her home. My friends used to tease me by saying that it took me "just" five years to walk this block and find my destiny.

When I met Valentine, she was eighteen years old. I was almost twenty-eight at that time. I already had the Army and seven years of work experience behind me. Valentine was in her second year at the Medical University in the city of Kazan, the capital of Tatarstan Republic. After we met, she transferred to Chishinev Medical University. She was preparing to become a doctor, like the previous two generations of her family. Her grandmother was a dentist, her father a surgeon, and her mother an eye doctor.

Her parents left the Medical University in order to go into World War II as doctors. They quickly became specialists at front line hospitals. They served during the whole war and then returned home.

When Valentine was 13 her father died from a heart attack. He was a proud man. It was impossible for him to tolerate the humiliating situation of Jewish doctors during Stalin's reign after the war. The period of Stalin's anti-Semitic policy was a terrible time. Stalin had always been suspicious of Jews, by 1949 he stopped hiding his hatred for them. The USSR voted for the creation of the country of Israel in the United Nations hoping that this new country would join the socialist countries. The American orientation of Israel caused such indignation in the USSR government that as a punishment, they decided to send all Jewish people to Siberia. By that time Stalin had already moved whole nations to other regions of the country, e. g., the Crimean Tatars, Kalmyks, Chechens. By 1953 temporary barracks were already built in Siberia. Local authorities had lists of people subject to immediate dispatch. Stalin searched for a justification to do this. The reason was soon found.

The most famous doctors of the country who had treated government leaders for three decades were accused of attempting to poison these elite patients. The phrase "Spies in white dress" spread to local newspapers and magazines from the major ones. That editorializing persuaded the people of the country in one day that a doctor with a Jewish background was a traitor to the Motherland and therefore not trustworthy enough to take care of people's health. Nobody wanted to be a patient of these doctors.

The mockery of Jewish doctors spread to other Jewish people irrespective of their job, but the doctors remained the focal point. Stalin knew the people well. He knew the deep historical roots of anti-Semitism. Stalin was the self proclaimed "Leader of all times", and on his appeal thousands of "patriots" in Russia, Ukraine, Moldova, and the other twelve republics were ready to destroy "ungrateful" Jewish people.

At that time I was seventeen years old. I remember the events of those disturbing days well. Dozens of the most celebrated doctors were maliciously blamed and tortured. Without any investigations thousands of them all over the

*My wife Valentine
and I as newlyweds.*

country were discharged from their offices. Valentine's father was relieved of his position. This affected him so deeply that he became seriously ill. He was just thirty-seven years old when he died.

When it seemed that no one and nothing could brighten that darkness, Stalin the dictator died. Among the first acts of the new government was a decision to stop the unreasonable barbarity against the whole Jewish nation. The chain of government decisions concerning Jewish people was canceled. However, that was only on the government level.

In real life remnants of anti-Semitism brought by these actions against doctors lingered for decades to come. Alone Valentine's mother supported Valentine and her sister Zhanna. Doctors were on one of the lower income levels in the USSR, but by working long hours, she was able to give them a University education.

Our wedding was a small one. Our families could not afford anything more. Valentine and I did not mind. We got married in Valentine's apartment on August 15, 1964; twenty-five people attended. We have been happily married ever since. We started our life together in a ten square yard room where there was nothing except a bed and a small table. Four years later we had a substantial income and a nice home. We could afford many things, including furniture, books, theater, and travel.

Valentine and I have a lot in common. We have always shared a lot of things. We have both always been involved with our son Henry. We both like books, theater, especially drama and ballet. Apart from my full-time job, I have always been involved in outside activities. That is why Valentine has always spent more time taking care of our home than I have. I am not handy around the house, while Valentine always has been. She can do everything from needlepoint to home repair. Before my wife entered the University, she worked as a draftsperson because she always had perfect handwriting. I never wrote neatly. Whenever it was necessary to complete any papers, I always depended upon my wife.

Big changes occurred in our lives after we immigrated to the United States in 1992. In moving, my wife and I naturally lost our jobs and our social status. That was frightening, especially for educated people. Unless you have lived through such an experience, you cannot possibly understand the feelings.

Valentine worked in a well-known dental clinic in Chishinev, the capital city of Moldova, for twenty five years. She was a well- respected dentist. People highly valued her skills and human qualities. She was considered to be as good a dentist as her grandmother, who had Leonid Brezhnev as one of her patients. Many prominent people were Valentine's patients as well. During those twenty five years of work, she treated about 100,000 thankful people.

Moving to the United States significantly affected our lives.

While the experience of being an immigrant often proves too difficult for the lives of many people, we are happy that it was not for us. Despite all the changes we have always kept our deep feelings and devotion to each other. I have a wonderful wife.

Our love for our son and grandchildren is also boundless. Children are our lives. I have sacrificed and will continue to sacrifice anything for their happiness. It seems to me that my children and grandchildren have the most loving, the most devoted, and the best mother and grandmother in the world.

The Old Professor: Back to Day Care

My life was an exception in my family and possibly in my whole town. It was an active, social, professional and productive life. I worked as a Department Head and Professor at the Academy of Sciences, the most prestigious scientific-research Institution in the former USSR. Since I spent so many years at the Academy I knew a lot of famous scientists and researchers of the country.

As the Vice President of the Union of Entrepreneurs, I met and worked with noted businessmen and governmental officials across the country. Since I also spent much time in the International Institute of Management for Eastern Europe, I was able to meet and work with highly experienced specialists from many countries. I loved my work and achieved recognition and success in science and business. Nevertheless, I chose to leave my country.

The growing unrest influenced me greatly. This included the tension between Moldovian, Ukrainian, Russian and Jewish people and the civil war there. These conflicts reminded me of my family's losses through years of wars and revolutions. I asked the United States to accept my family as refugees.

To our great pleasure the Department of Immigration

replied positively to my inquiry. We moved to America in December 1992. We are thankful for the financial, moral, and medical support we received, and we are grateful for the rights that every American citizen enjoys.

For thirty-eight years I worked professionally in the USSR. I left not only my country but also all my property, research work, and the right to retirement benefits. Behind me I left a comfortable home with nice furniture, paintings, and library. Although I published three of my seven books in 1992, because of inflation my comensation ended up with little value. Now I am like my ancestors: a financially challenged man. But the most terrifying things were becoming dependent in matters large and small, and an almost absolute social isolation.

Becoming a U.S. Citizen

The main obstacle was my difficulty with the English language. In spite of the fact that I could read, write, and speak four other languages; I at once became blind, deaf and mute. looking at books or newspapers and seeing nothing except unknown letters, or listening to the radio and TV but understanding nothing and not being able to speak a word. I was forced by these new circumstances to start my life from the very beginning again.

Through different periods of history my family of three generations, regardless of our abilities and professions (farmer, worker, doctor, scientist) ended up the same. Similar to us are millions of people who could not change their destiny.

One was not able to complete building his house; the other could not finish writing his book; the third could not see the first harvest of his recently planted garden; the fourth could not complete his engineering project, etc. Although they lived in a country with rich natural resources and although they were talented, they were not lucky enough to live their lives with amenities, even over a one hundred year time span.

Chapter 13

An Outsider, Out But Not Down

Great changes have occurred in my life. I am an immigrant. In the USA immigration is not new. With the exception of the Native American, one is either an immigrant or a descendant of one.

However, times change. From the beginning the government supports immigrants financially in a way that two decades ago would have been a dream. The average immigrant has also changed. Over 50% of immigrants from Eastern European countries are people with some higher education and the educational level of contemporary immigrants is much higher than their predecessors. Because of this, the period of adaptation to life in the new country has become shorter. One hundred years ago an immigrant needed at least twenty-five years, a whole generation, to adapt to American life. After World War II that period became half of that. Presently this period has been halved again and is now about six years.

According to the data of a Research Institute of the New Americas, 80% of people who have been in the United States for six or more years have a job. Of these, half have an annual income of more than $40,000. Eleven percent have an annual income in excess of $75,000. These statistics represent hundreds of thousands of people.

Most immigrants can be categorized into three groups. The first group has a high level of education and professional knowledge and speaks English well. These people are able to quickly find jobs. A second group cannot speak English well and has inadequate education and work experience. A third group includes people who have been professionals such as doctors, engineers, teachers, scientists, musicians, etc. with years of work experience in another country. They are older and do not know English well enough to communicate effectively.

For every immigrant, each step in a new country is difficult. The process of adaptation to new living conditions, a new culture, traditions, the style of behavior, etc. takes tremendous effort. The first and second groups join American society quickly, the only difference being that the first group gets higher positions and salaries. For the third group, age combined with poor English language skills exclude much chance of getting a meaningful job. This is an extremely difficult situation.

Most Americans, even if they were born in the United States, at age fifty-five or older usually do not try to build a new career despite having studied and worked here for decades because they know the labor laws and understand life in this country. Immigrants who may be professionally well-educated are often absolutely unprepared to work in the same field in the US.

In their former countries after working many years, giving everything they were capable of and overcoming great difficulties, they achieved recognition in a field of industry, science, medicine, education, art, etc. In a new country, their professional experience and knowledge are not too useful to the society.

Who is now interested in the fact that a particular immigrant was a good doctor, experienced engineer, honored economist, an excellent teacher or musician, a creator of new type of cognac, or the author of a new method for cold welding metals in the past? We have become "dinosaurs."

I am one of these immigrants. Computers have helped make many of my skills archaic. Familiar techniques have become obsolete. Certain skills developed in a socialist society are outmoded in America. Many functions are simply done differently here. Popular careers in programming, finance, and parts of physics, biology, and mathematics attract younger professionals. The older generation is more distant from them.

These superannuated professionals are able to work but are too old by American standards and cannot be accepted in most jobs. They do their best to be useful to their families and their new Motherland. They would be glad to have any kind of job. But nobody takes them seriously. Who would like to teach people in their sixties to work in a company or office? They have language problems and do not know the details of such jobs. It does not matter if they can learn a new job in a short period of time or whether their knowledge and experience will make them better workers.

Employers tend to ignore the resumes of this group of immigrants. The economics professor who knows English fairly well cannot even get a job as a bookkeeper. The artist once recognized as one of the best in the former USSR is denied a job painting three blocks in white, red and green repetitively. The dentist with twenty-five years of experience cannot get a job as a dental hygienist, even with US certification for that position.

Many of my personal friends and myself have received such explanations as: "We are impressed with your general knowledge and experience, but we are looking for a person with more experience in this particular field"; "You are overqualified for this job"; "The other candidates have work experience in the United States," etc. But they cannot gain this experience if no one will hire them.

Somebody once said that there are three reasons to use language: to express thoughts, to hide thoughts, and to speak instead of having any thoughts.

During my first years in America I tried to understand the logic of such answers from prospective employers. I realized that these answers are masterpieces of bureaucratic writing. They are simply a way to ignore an older person's efforts to get a job. The company uses phrases such as "your outstanding knowledge" as it denies a low-paying job. This is the reality that we must accept.

Unemployed workers receive an even greater shock when, after investigating advertisements for job openings, they discover that company "A" has claimed bankruptcy, company "B" is laying off a quarter of their workforce, and company "C" has not hired anybody in several years. The vacancy announcements were really intended to persuade others of the company's well-being. There are no jobs, and there will not likely be any in the near future.

Not only does unemployment create financial problems, but if immigrants' knowledge and experience are not in use, a previously unknown feeling of uselessness develops inside them. This is the most terrible experience of all. The more educated you are, the higher your professional level, and the more significant your career achievement, the more frightening this feeling becomes.

Family Relations

Yesterday you were the head of a family who taught your children and acted as their most important advisor and major financial supporter. Today your children see you confused and unconfident. You know little and understand even less about this new life. In a short time you have changed from the head of the family to a dependant. You do not know what is good or bad in our new country. You understand little when speaking on the phone. You cannot communicate with the doctor or the office staff. You cannot go to the store by yourself, as you have never driven a car before.

In addition to this, you can do little to influence the circumstances of your children's lives. In most situations you become dependent on them.

Our children's lives are no easier than our own were at the beginning. They have had to work, study, and struggle for a place in life. They have had to adapt quickly to a new culture, traditions, and styles of behavior. All this depends on them having a good knowledge of the language, which is accomplished through hard work every day. They only have themselves to depend on. No one is available to give good advice, and they have no old and devoted friends with experience near them.

Young people are always busy. Needs and requests of elders are not important and make them miserable. The generation gap between parents and children comes to its broadest point. To have worthy family relations members of different generations should have lots of tact and patience. For immigrants this is much more complex. Some families deal with this well and some, unfortunately, do not.

Relations with Others

How to build relations with people in a different country must be learned. This is primarily due to the difference in culture.

In the former Soviet Union, for example, the most prevailing topics of conversation were the country's international situation, the political situations within the country, staff changes within the government, and literature.

In the United States people are busy with their own problems and global questions are left to those who are responsible for dealing with them. Many Americans, of course, very well understand the situation in this country and abroad. They know well the situation in Iraq or Afghanistan, Chechnya, or the Republics of the former Yugoslavia. They have vivid discussions about freedom of the press and publicity in China. Regardless, domestic problems are more important to Americans than world problems. In spite of the fact that each day the interdependence of countries grows. What happens in economics and in the market directly in one place influences other places around the world. The average American has ignored this. The tragic events of September 11, 2001, were an awakening.

In Europe there is more open discussion and involvement in such things as politics, literature, and the theater among a broad range of citizens. Many Americans are preoccupied with cinema and soap operas. While the cultural differences are many, the main obstacle for an immigrant is the language barrier. In Russia everything was much easier.

I knew Russian and Western literature, music, art, and the international and the domestic situations well. I traveled extensively within the former USSR. Because of this I knew a lot of interesting stories about Moscow, St. Petersburg, Latvia, Lithuania, Central Asia, the Caucasus republics, the Ural area, Siberia, the northern parts of the country, as well as Ukraine and Moldova. No language barriers got in the way of expressing opinions. Now almost nothing of these past experiences are interesting to people in my new big country. As of yet I do not know much about this country, but I have worked very hard to learn about the history, culture, and current events of the United States. With a limited capability for using the English language I cannot share my views as I did in my native country. Often my "broken language" makes it difficult to get close to other people.

Relations with Friends

It was not easy to realize that even relationsips between people are based on something different in a new country. In addition to fundamental criteria such as personality, ethics, mutual interest, etc., there are differences in establishing a friendship in the United states. In America friendship is often based on ones financial status. This is quite understandable. Friends often travel together, visit each other at home, go out together, or are involved in a common activity.

After I moved to America, I had a few meetings with a Vice President of the Xerox Corporation. I was seeking a job, so I tried to show him my abilities. Probably my knowledge and experiences were interesting to him. One day he asked his assistant to help me fill out the necessary papers to become a member of a prestigious private club. I found out that the annual membership was twice my income at that time. I found a way to refuse his proposal without embarrassing either of us.

Finance also impacted my lifestyle in the former USSR,

but in a more restricted way. Quite different, for example, were the apartments and holiday conditions for laborers, collective farmers, and construction workers from those of representatives of the government or managers of organizations. There the high salaries were only four or five times those of the lower ones.

The CEO of a company or a university professor's salary was five hundred rubles per month, a skilled worker's was around two hundred, and a teacher or a doctor's was one hundred and fifty. The lowest workers were paid about one hundred per month.

In America the income range is significantly broader. Thus there is a wide difference in houses and common "toys" such as swimming pools, club memberships, cottages, boats and cars. Some have private air-planes, big yachts, and multiple residences. These were almost unheard of in the former USSR. While people's financial status is only one of many factors that support or destroy friendships, it is the most significant one.

I have witnessed many such examples during the past ten years, long-time friendships between people were lost. During the early 1970's I knew two young people who had always been together, as they studied at the same University and worked in the same organization. They helped each other and spent their vacation time together with their families. Twenty-five years ago, one immigrated to the US. He was able to find a good career. His friend came to America just seven years ago, much older than his friend had been when immigrating.

The second has had great financial and morale problems in his period of adaptation to his new country. Years earlier in the USSR, this second person financially helped the first. He let the first live in his apartment for two years for free and helped in many other ways. Now the first is cold toward his former friend. His advice and comments are more painful than the sting of a bee. It is not that he should financially support the other person, or give him an apartment or work. But unfortunately, he does not even show simple sympathy or understanding of his friend's situation. The reason is simply the financial success of the one and the unluckiness of the other. Both still have a lot in common, are seriously involved in sports and books, and have a sense of humor. But they were not able to save their friendship.

I once knew a man who was well-educated and gifted who worked in the same field of science as I did, although we lived in different cities. The more often I met him at the institute where he worked, the more I realized that his colleagues did not treat him with respect. That surprised me. Later I realized that he was the one of those people who always overestimated his own importance among co-workers and valued only his own work and opinions. If it were to his benefit, he would betray his colleagues.

In 1989 he had received a two-year contract to work in a Western European country.

In 1993 I was looking through a specialized magazine and found an article written by him. I also learned that he held a respected position. I thought about calling him. He had known me for many years, and I thought he might recommend me as a potential employee to some companies where my knowledge and experience could be helpful. But, knowing his personality, I had doubts about contacting him.

Six months later, one of our mutual friends told him that I was in America. Our friend subsequently recommended that I call the man. When I called, he invited me to a meeting with business people from the Ukraine and Moldova. I accepted his invitation, as I had worked with many of those people before.

After the meeting I gave him my résumé and asked for his help. I soon found he had no credibility. According to him, he found a job two hours after arriving in New York City. He said he had tried to help some immigrants. A few days before, he claimed, he had given a check for five hundred dollars to one of his former colleagues. I was skeptical about that statement, as I had heard jokes about his greediness. Leaving him, I felt disappointed. I knew he would not help me. I also suspected that the next time he met someone we both knew, he would tell them that two former Ph.D. professors had recently visited him, and that he had given each of them a check for five hundred dollars. Unfortunately, I was not mistaken.

Out But Not Down

Since my early childhood, I have always known the value of time. Growing up and gaining more responsibilities, I was sometimes not able to "steal" an extra half hour for rest. That is why it was so difficult for me when, for the first time in my life, I had plenty of free time and no way to spend it constructively.

The main obstacle was my difficulty with the English language. Living as an outsider is frightening because it is almost impossible to find a way out of the situation. It takes years to learn how to read, speak, and write in a different language, and because I began later in life, it was even harder. As a result, my feelings of isolation and hopelessness were long-term.

During this time I lost a lot of what people valued in me—

my professionalism and my ability to understand and operate in life around me. My thoughts, my ideas, my dreams—I couldn't express any of them. The past was gone, the present was terrible, and the future offered little hope. Everything worked against me. I was learning the language more slowly than expected, and my professional knowledge and experience was becoming more outdated with each day. I was unable to continue my traveling on the "main street" of life. I was stopped, possibly forever.

I doubted that I could ever recover my past way of life. Everyone wants to live comfortably, but pride and career are not the only goals. My needs were much deeper.

A scientist will always be a scientist. During my three decades in the field I had received many scientific and honorary diplomas and certificates and had held high positions. Like most scientists I had a peculiar way of thinking about and understanding the world around me. It became an important part of my identity. This, combined with my many unsuccessful attempts to establish a career, made life extremely difficult.

Every morning I woke up with the same unpleasant thoughts about my life. Often I just tried to hide from everyone and everything. Moreover, I tried to hide from myself. How could I save the person I truly was? How could I shake off my depression? In the words of a philosopher, "If there is no hope, no goal in life, you have to invent it." I think I have been quite successful in this.

During the first years in the United States I kept up-to-date on the projects prepared by reliable economic institutions for Russia and other former republics of the USSR. I learned more about US companies involved in that area then offered my professional help as a volunteer to a few of these companies. This lasted for two years. I did not get paid, but I expanded my circle of acquaintances. That work allowed me to stay in a good professional shape as well.

After participating in three projects, I mentioned getting paid for my work. I was told plainly that for the salary the company would need to pay to me, they could find ten scientists living outside of the United States who would be willing to work as contractors. Although I understood, it was hard for me to believe that even big successful companies welcomed the services of those who agreed to work for nothing. I found a similar situation in the academic field. I gave some lectures as a guest professor and was also a scientific editor of articles about the Economics of Russia. In some works I was recognized and thanked, but in others I found nothing.

Later I did volunteer work at a library, then lectured as a teacher of the Russian language. But my most important survival tactic was quite different.

First, I tried to convince myself that I was ten years older than I really was. A person's needs decrease with age. With this attitude I learned to accept the little I had.

Second, I adopted the philosophy that "nothing can be absolutely positive or absolutely negative in life." Therefore, I reasoned, there must be something positive in my situation. The important thing was to find it.

Soon I realized that the only positive left in my life besides my family was my ability to learn more about the world. To me, nothing in life gives more satisfaction and joy than creative work, new knowledge, and discoveries. The discovery does not need to be of global importance; it might only involve "discovery" of myself. The process of learning is endless. Pursuing this, I was soon able to make judgments about issues of different scientific branches almost on a satisfying level. My knowledge was increasing, and I felt almost like a happy person. But it couldn't last.

I don't remember how it happened, but one day, looking through my many writings and notes, I started to compare my archives of knowledge with a warehouse of a good things stored up and gone to waste. What use are these things if they benefit no one? What use is knowledge if there is nobody to share it with and no possibility of using it yourself? I came to the conclusion that it was time to create a new life goal for myself. This book is a part of my new hopes.

Chapter 14

Who am I ?

For centuries, my forefathers lived in a small town in the Ukraine. Old Jewish traditions and religious rites were strictly passed on from generation to generation. The common languages were Ukrainian and Yiddish. Only the men could speak Ukrainian at any functional level. By nature the townspeople were plain, honest, and highly trusting. Time passed. Older generations were replaced by the younger, but for centuries their way of life did not change.

No common thread bound these people to the rest of the world. They lived far from the railroad and the industrial centers, and the only method of transportation was by horse. They did not read books or newspapers, and in fact only the children of the wealthy were taught to read and write at all. Institutions of higher learning were closed to them. Medical services existed only in the imagination. Interaction with people outside the town was limited. Marriages between cousins were common. It sometimes seemed that time had stopped. No world events could disrupt or alter this God-ordained, unchanging way of life except for frequent wars, revolutions, and pogroms, which destroyed and exterminated almost everything, including the lives of thousands of people.

But those who survived toiled, and, step by step, rebuilt their homes, revived their businesses and trades, and reestablished their centuries old way of life.

Significant Changes

At the beginning of the 20th century much began to change. People began to believe that revolution could rid them of tsarist repression and guarantee liberty and equality to people of different creeds. Activists eliminated the *kulaks* (the richest owners of land), created agricultural cooperatives, and forced industrialization of the country. In doing so, they ignored the impact of all this on the average citizen. People here did not involve themselves in politics and as a result, the evil hand of Stalinist repression touched only a few.

Unfortunately, among these victims was my uncle Gregory who used to work for a Moscow newspaper. In 1939 he perished in Stalin's camp. My only knowledge of him is that he gave me a generous and uncommon gift at that time, a tricycle. I know because my father told me about it.

After World War II almost 70% of the Jewish male population of the town did not return from the battlefields. The late 1940s and early 50s saw the worst of governmental anti-Semitism. Like generations before people felt that something menacing was advancing towards them. But, like their forefathers, they kept on working and silently waited for their fate. This time, fate smiled upon them. Stalin died, and Khrushchev's "thaw" arrived.

Young people left for big cities, some to learn, others to work, some for both. They built different lives for themselves but something common united them.

They lived and worked in a multicultural society in conditions where any mention of religion could mean severe punishment from the government. A friend of mine was expelled from the University of Kazan, Tatarstan, because someone saw a religious book in his briefcase. Atheism became prevalent and affected everybody. Young Jewish people were more vulnerable than other ethnic groups and thus more susceptible to ideas of internationalism and atheism. They were far away from their families and their culture and constantly feared condemnation from other nationalities and accusation of loyalty to the Zionist movement. They began to forget the language their parents spoke along with their religion and the traditions of their people.

After two generations of life in such conditions, a Jew by birth and in soul, raised in Russian, Georgian, Lithuanian, Uzbek, etc. culture, began to characterize himself by the term "Jew-not Jew."

In that country and at that time it was thought quite normal that a well educated Jew who was otherwise conversant with books, plays, art, and the like could hardly name scarcely more than a single Jewish book, play, song, or work of art. This became so deeply ingrained in our character that the majority of middle and older age immigrants from the former USSR, having lived ten or more years in the USA, still could not fully become part of the American Jewish community. There are many reasons for this, but the most significant appears to be that Americans cannot fathom the depths of the tragedy that befell the spiritual life of Jews in the former Communist nations. Because of this lack of understanding, there appears to be an irritation and even disenchantment with us.

Immigration

Upon coming to America, I went to lectures on Judaism, read on the subject with great interest, and attended the synagogue, although not regularly. But I often realize that I am not able to accept much on faith. I am also constantly analyzing everything in the light of my past knowledge and experience. This is a long and arduous process related to changes in outlook and values appropriated decades ago under quite different historical and cultural circumstances. At the same time it's very interesting. It's like people who don't know or like music and thus cannot appreciate how much they are missing. This applies in even greater measure to people who have been deprived of a great moral and religious tradition, or who have discarded principles of ethnic and national identity.

Something curious and enlightening happened to me one spring day in 1994. A Professor of Sociology from Rochester Institute of Technology invited my family for a religious holiday evening.

He was at the head of the table and conducted the evening ably, strictly following the rules corresponding to this event. It all was new to me. I carefully followed his every move and word, delighted in his erudition and knowledge of these customs that were alien to me. But the main actors that evening were his children about three to eight years old. The eyes of each sparkled with some sort of special flame; they knew everything by heart and sometimes got ahead of their father in the ritual, imbuing it with animation and joy. I truly envied this splendid family, whose members were so free and real in the religion of their people, as they followed the rites and rituals of their forefathers.

Of course, many believe that a person's pride of heritage

and how he follows the ethical norms of his people is much more important than how he observes traditional rituals. Early in the 20th century Turkey entered Armenia and massacred a half a million of their people. This tragic event affects not only those who survived but every succeeding generation, becoming an integral part of the personality of Armenians. Similarly, memories like this are part of the Native American's personality. In like manner an inherent part of modern day Judaism is the memory and feeling for the Holocaust tragedy. That experience is vivid to me. Who better than people who experienced the Holocaust in real life and survived it could better understand it? Emotionally, this was a special evening for me. I recognized anew that what had happened was our misfortune and not our fault.

We lived in a country with no freedom of religion, where religious people were persecuted. There were restrictions in the choice of a profession and in employment. Sometimes people were severely punished since religious practice was deemed to be a crime against the regime. This lasted for decades. It shouldn't be surprising that the process of adapting to the historical roots of one's religion, is much slower than adapting to American culture. But I am an optimist. I am convinced that time will put everything in its place, that life will correct this iniquity in the fate of my people.

Homeland

In the former USSR patriotic feelings toward the nation were most often expressed with the word Motherland. For the majority of the population, especially the younger ones, this word signified pride in their nation, loyalty to its interests, and willingness to lay down their lives for its independence. With age these patriotic feelings were subjected to periodic revision in some circles of the populace. The people loved their big, resource and talent-rich country, it's nature, and centuries-old traditions and culture. But they also feared it, or rather they feared the dictators who for decades ruled the nation and its life, unaccountable to the interests and freedoms of individuals.

They feared its laws, which could be used by tyrants against them. They were afraid of the follies of local governments who could do essentially whatever they wanted. They feared the unpredictability of life in which periodic attempts of government to break negative tendencies in the economy always ended up crashing and burning. They could not understand why the authorities couldn't or wouldn't see the tremendous technological and economic changes taking place in the USA, Western Europe, and Southeast Asia and make corresponding decisions.

Love and fear, or fear and love, for the country in which you were born were always near.

However, even if circumstances forced you to emigrate from your country, it doesn't mean that ties are absolutely cut to your previous land and life or special memories left behind. You will never forget places of your childhood, the school or university where you studied, colleagues, and neighbors with whom you worked and lived for many years.

It is difficult to acknowledge that you can never meet old friends because life has scattered us throughout the world, or to understand that no one will ever call to remind you of traditional reunions with your former university classmates. It is painful to realize that chance meetings with acquaintances and close friends, some of whom you hiked with in the mountains of the former USSR, or explored the deserts of Central Asia, or visited the gas and oil producing regions of

Northern Siberia, or gave lectures to workers beyond the Arctic Circle, are forever lost.

By far the most painful feeling for me, however, are the new circumstances that prevent me from visiting places that are holy to me—the graves of my parents. Only every seven or eight years will I be able to visit the burial place of my mother who gave me life, buried in the Ukraine, my mother who raised me, buried in Israel, or my father, a relationship that was most special in my life, buried in Moldova. No matter how many years I live in a country that is new to me and no matter what life I build, I will never forget this separation. Millions of people could tell you the same.

In a new country, people undergo profound changes. Without doubt, from the first minute of arrival in America, the immigrant is immensely grateful to the country that saved his life and protected him from potential tragedy. He appreciates the land that gave him haven, extended material, medical, and other kinds of help to prepare him for life and work. Most impressive to me is the comprehensive support for the older people.

These people have worked for other countries thirty-five to fifty years on farms, in factories, schools, colleges, banks, railroads, barber shops, etc. But the republics of the former Soviet Union because of poverty and a host of other reasons do not pay their elderly a penny of pension.

It's not surprising that in immigrants family celebrations a toast to their new country, "God bless America," has become a tradition. You develop a sense of loyalty to the USA. You begin to understand better the life, the reasons for economic and technological progress in this country, the superiority of its laws and freedoms, its history and the beauty of its nature. Finally, you begin to be proud of this country, proud even though you may not be as significant part of it as you would like, but, nevertheless, you are still a part of it.

This feeling of homeland towards the new country comes differently to each person. One person needs more time than another.

My son, for example, soon after emigrating visited Moldova. On the third day he phoned and told me he wanted to come home to the USA.

For the older generation this process takes somewhat longer. One morning, after being here two and a half years, my wife told me she had a nightmare in which she was back in the USSR. Fortunately, to her great relief she "woke up" in the USA. The main thing is that even on a subconscious level the new immigrant becomes aware that the new country is not merely a place of residence but a Homeland.

After six years in the USA I became a citizen of this great land. It was a special day for me. That day was a culmination of what many generations of my family dreamed about. And yet with great love for them and with memories of each, I thought of my children and future generations of my family in those minutes. Each one of them is guaranteed freedom and equal rights in life, which can really be valued by one who was at one time denied them.

Reading this, I once again ask myself, Who am I now? I can't find an answer convincing enough for myself. Everything is so complex. I am a Jew by birth, Ukrainian by place of birth, Russian by language and culture, and a citizen of the USA. I am seriously trying to learn the language, culture, and laws of my new country as well as understand the American view of life. Additionally, I am at the same time educated and uneducated. Although I hold two doctoral degrees, I will never understand thousands of questions that would seem obvious to a child born in the USA. I am a professional who worked over thirty years as an economist and not a professional because a former Soviet economist has no standing in America. I am trained to use my brain and completely untrained in doing things with my hands, a person with ideas and at the same time too old by American standards to implement them. It becomes clear there is much dichotomy in one person.

Sometimes it seems to me I have more life experiences than an average American does. I have lived in countries with different social orders. I found out through real life, not through books, what Fascism is, and have experienced fear, hunger, cold, insult, life on the edge and the deaths of those close to me. I had to overcome great obstacles on my way to earning a higher education and then pursuing my academic career. I lived many years in republics with different cultures (Ukraine, Moldova, Uzbekistan, Kazakhstan) and regions with various religious traditions—Orthodox, Protestant, Catholic, Muslim. I have had some unique life opportunities. And isn't this a unique experience of not only observing but deeply feeling in myself tremendous changes in society including the disintegration of the vast, seemingly impervious, Soviet empire.

I lost everything, including both property and social status, that I had won through many decades of hard work. In my new country I experienced a full devaluation of my diplomas and certificates. There was no demand for my knowledge and experience. I have lived through the tribulations of the first steps in the life of an immigrant. They have all left an imprint on my view of the world.

I have many acquaintances and friends in America, including many who were born here. Yet I often realize we see things differently.

I believe that I take a broader approach towards events and solutions to many political, economic, social, and national problems because of bitter experiences in my former country. Often when I am discussing a problem, I discover that I know more about adjoining aspects of the subject than an American. Conversely, an American-born citizen tends to be much more aware of the details of the subject. For an American there are no trivial things. If a person is an expert in something, he or she knows the subject completely. This attention to detail and the constant striving to do a better job today than yesterday is one of the major advantages of an American specialist and one of the deciding factors in progress as a whole in the USA. Miscalculation of this has cost me dearly.

So who am I? I am not confident in my ability to answer this question effectively. On one hand there is my family history in the former Soviet Union. But my children and grandchildren live in America.

I try to evaluate myself in six fundamental components of my identity: nationality, religion, culture, morals, love for Homeland, and view of the world. Apparently, I am a necessary link between my forefathers and my children and future generations of my family not only in a biological sense but also in a historical and social sense. I, as many others, am a person in transition. I am a person, whom the whims of fate did not allow to sing until the end of his old song. Now it is too late to learn to sing flawlessly a new one. While I may not be able to reconstruct myself completely, I will try to do my best. But the most significant point here is that my children and grandchildren already feel themselves a free people in our great country, the United States of America.

Chapter 15

FINDING WHILE LOSING

What noble people we have discovered in the United States!

From our first days in our new country many people have helped us. Our relatives rented a one bedroom apartment for us and bought a bed, a table, and some chairs. Someone gave us an old couch, another donated an armchair, and yet another gave us a lamp. These gifts were especially touching because they were so unexpected. We had to overcome decades of deeply rooted stereotypes about Americans. We had been taught that Americans were interested only in themselves. What a pleasant surprise we found. Instead of selfish Americans, we met kind-hearted people sincerely trying to help immigrants get used to their new lives in the USA. Their kindness was particularly important to building our morale.

Two years before we moved I had the opportunity to visit America. I met many people, including businessmen and scientists, whom I still gratefully count among my closest friends. They include a former Deputy Attorney of the State of Pennsylvania—Bob and his wonderful wife Peggy—and Jacob, a farmer, and his wife Mabel. These friends visited us in the Soviet Union and were a part of our "old" life.

A few weeks after I moved to the US, I contacted these friends and they came to visit my family in Rochester. They were the only people in America who knew me as a successful scientist and businessman in the USSR. Hence, they knew how to advise me and could tell me what to expect in this new life situation. Their advice and encouragement meant much to us at that time. Even today our reunions give us many pleasant hours, and our conversations routinely extend well into the night.

Bob and Peggy gave us subscriptions to *National Geographic* and the *Smithsonian* magazines, which at first I did not understand, because at that time I did not know there were such magazines. I understood later that these gifts were thoughtful gestures of friendship. They knew we would appreciate these wonderful magazines. When I thanked them, I also disclosed my weakness and deep affection for books.

Another group of special people we discovered was the professional teachers of the English language in adult education programs. They were not only teachers of English, but our cultural guides in our new world. For months we looked at America through the eyes of our teacher. We just did not have any other viewpoint in those early days.

Teachers changed about every two months. All of them were wonderful in different ways. My first teacher worked hard until finally we began to understand each other. If the meaning of the words was unclear to us, he would create an artistic performance just for the situation, and which would help us understand. Our second teacher achieved the desired results using a totally different approach. My third teacher used music as his medium. He sang well, and often taught us English by singing patriotic and American folks songs. The next, a former baseball player, offered a good sense of US history with a special focus on politics and economics. And, of course, he taught us about baseball as a part of American culture. We had many wonderful teachers.

Each of our teachers was different, but together there was an unrivaled synergy that greatly helped us acquire language, customs, and culture in the US. I will always be thankful that all of my teachers treated us with dignity and respect. As people struggling in a new society, we will always be grateful for the way they supported us in those early days.

Before my immigration I had no idea how prevalent volunteer activities were among Americans. We discovered many people, including complete strangers, who were eager to reach out to those in need with their time, goods, and talents. They seemed naturally driven to help. They were in the streets, nursing homes, stores, schools, libraries, and fire departments. They seemed to be everywhere. We found many volunteers who helped immigrants learn English and American culture, opening the way to an independent life. What could be more critical for someone just arriving at their new Homeland? What noble people we discovered!

The first volunteer to help me was Jane, a college teacher. Regardless of weather, transportation difficulties, or other personal circumstances, we conversed and studied every Tuesday at 7:00 PM. Jane was a language specialist, who taught aspiring writers and lecturers. Despite my scant fifty-word English vocabulary, each of our meetings started with encouraging words: "How quickly you are progressing in English. "Good work!" These words leave me in utter amazement but I keep my silence. There have been only a few times in my life when I have been overwhelmed by my inability to accomplish the task before me. This was one of them.

These meetings with Jane were a major life event for me. Learning the new language was so difficult that I felt like I was running up a sand dune, going up two steps and sliding back one.

In spite of my personal fears and feelings of failure, Jane's professional drive overcame my fears. We gradually expanded the discussion topics from my family to life in the former USSR, and from my first simple Ukrainian job to my work in science. We talked about our little immigrants' enclave in Rochester and about the larger situation of immigrants in America. I regarded my time with Jane as a beacon of light in a world of darkness.

As a volunteer with a group of Americans whom I helped to improve their Russian language skills, I met a man named David. David asked me a few simple questions that were enough to show me that he was a serious student of Russian. After our regular group time passed, I continued my conversation with David. We agreed that it would be beneficial for both of us to meet and speak both in English and in Russian. Our meetings soon became regular. I have to admit that David soon suggested that we spend more of our time together on my English than his Russian. As we continued our teamwork, David's life unfolded before me .

David was a bachelor in his fifties who worked as a plumber. His job was physical and demanded overtime work. He seldom took a vacation. There were many things I learned to like about David, but I was most impressed by his high intellect. He not only knew US history, but he was equally well-versed in politics, economics, and literature. In addition to English and Russia, he also spoke Spanish, French, and some Vietnamese. Our relationship grew as we learned more and more about each other. The only topic that seemed closed to discussion was his former job.

David had spent his earlier years at a college as Director of Foreign Language Studies. Because he was open about so many other parts of his life, I knew he had serious reasons for protecting his privacy in this area. Actually, one of his friends once divulged that David's encyclopedic knowledge had frequently irritated some of his colleagues. Another of his friends admitted that there had been other problems. Even now I do not know what really happened. However, I truly believe that hundreds of students lost a very gifted language teacher when David left the college. They also lost the gift of his broad educational background, which he freely interspersed with his language teaching.

Suddenly, darkness invaded our growing friendship. At fifty-three, David was stricken by a fatal heart attack while at work. People who had been close to him prepared a memorial booklet including about 150 philosophical aphorisms. David would have liked this. Reading it, I was reminded why I liked him so much. Until the very last moment of his life, David wanted to learn. When I think of him, I have one regret. If it were possible to go back in time, I would refuse some of the time he shared with me to let him rest at least one extra hour.

There are other people on my list of dedicated volunteers.

Laura holds an important position at the City School District, and was President of the Rochester Rotary Club and an active member of several additional volunteer organizations. One can easily imagine her busy schedule. But when I needed her help as a specialist in English or as an interpreter, she often managed to find the necessary time.

I was also amazed by the commitment of Tom, another

volunteer on my behalf. At the time he was a man in his early thirties, a father of three children with two jobs. In spite of these demands on his time, for three months he helped me and other immigrants in a variety of ways, from translating different letters to the preparation of our first resume in the USA.

Thanks mostly to these people, I gained access to American language, culture, and history. Within six months of my arrival I made my first trip to an American library. This was very exciting for me. In my past I had routinely visited the major libraries of Moscow, St. Petersburg, Paris, and Budapest. Libraries have always been almost holy places for me, so reaching this milestone was especially rewarding.

Another six months later I gave my first lecture in English at a local university. Then I published my first article in an American professional journal. I have also been privileged to do consulting work for some American corporations and institutions. I am truly grateful for all those who gave of themselves to help new Americans in their transition into a new culture and lifestyle.

Mike, a smart, attentive, warm-hearted person, was a volunteer who became a close friend. After he completed his university studies, he worked in various management positions in industry for many years. He has three children, whom he put through college. He loves his grandchildren. I know his three brothers, who live in different parts of the US, and I have developed a friendship with the youngest, Jim. I soon found that Mike had excellent knowledge of literature, politics, and history. From a young age, his life had been dedicated to the pursuit of knowledge. This included the study of the economics as well as the culture and traditions of the different nations of the former USSR. Long active in community service, Mike has held numerous positions in volunteer leadership, including his role as President of a Lions Club. He has many friends and acquaintances, and is loved and respected by all of them.

I met Mike in the most casual way. I was walking on a quiet street and greeted a man who was busy in his yard preparing wood for his fireplace. In response to my greeting, he said he needed a break from his labors and that led us into a conversation. We had talked about five minutes when he invited me to join him for a cup of coffee. I was surprised, but after a second invitation I could not refuse. He was naturally kind. We started to have phone conversations, then started to meet frequently. Now it is hard for me to imagine my life in America without him.

Mike and I discussed all sorts of questions. He gave me help and advice about different life situations. From him I learned about bills, letter writing, translating or reviewing materials before submitting them for publication, and more.

Mike has a very understanding personality. Sometimes I didn't have to explain anything to him. He just sensed that something was wrong, and his friendly optimism and support gave me hope for the future. He paid so much attention to my problems that once I told him that our friendship reminds me of a one-sided football game. He disagreed with my analogy, telling me that by communicating with me he was also expanding his education by seeing things afresh through my European eyes. I took his words as a joke. If I could only give him a small part of what he has given me, I would be very happy. I am so pleased that I found a sincere friend in my new country. Sometimes it is difficult to understand how Mike and I have become such close friends.

In childhood, friendships are spontaneous and uncalculated. We simply like a person, and that is enough. Friendship between adults is seldom free from considerations of personal interests. It is not just that one person enjoys the other's company, but also he can identify with his friend's social position, friends, financial situation, and so on.

The older we get, the more difficult it seems to form real connections with friends.

I have not developed my English skills well enough to communicate freely in America, and my knowledge of American culture is limited, too. My friendship with Mike became real not only because we have so many common interests and values, but because our personalities are actually complementary. At least this is what I think. I am fortunate to have Mike as my friend, and am truly lucky to have met so many good people in my new life in the United States.

I do not mean to paint a Pollyannaish picture of life in America. There are unscrupulous people in every country, and the United States is no exception. However, I have learned that Americans are generally hardworking and spiritual people, and "middle class" people, like the dozens I have met, are the basis of a healthy and sound American society.

The changes and challenges I have encountered since moving to the U.S. have had a profound influence on me as an individual. I have lost much of my past life. I lost my property, job, and social status, my culture, language, and friends. I no longer have the things that made me feel comfortable when I thought of home.

But here in America, fulfilling the dreams of several generations of my family, I found a new and beautiful homeland that gave me its hand of support during one of the most difficult periods of my life. If I have gained a little more wisdom, been a little more attentive to people, offered more kindness, and generally become a little better person than I was before, I owe thanks to the people I have introduced in this chapter and to so many others.

In my new country I have become enriched with novel experiences of life and freedom. I have new friends, a new culture, a new language, and a totally new outlook of life. I have great faith and hope for my children, grandchildren, and future generations of my family. All of this gives me great peace of mind.

A Rewarding Future

My son Henry was twenty-five when we moved to the United States. He has tried to find his place in this country of possibility and opportunity. He received a university education in the former USSR, where he studied economics and computer programming and then spent two years working for a private company. From his first days in the USA he started to look for a job, but all his attempts were unsuccessful.

After a year of job hunting, Henry decided to get an American college education at the William Simon Business School of the University of Rochester.

As a student he faced the common challenges of a new immigrant—language difficulties, cultural adjustments, and financial problems. An additional challenge was the birth of his first daughter, Ilene. By working fifteen to sixteen hours a day, he graduated with his Master's degree in Business Administration in one and a half years. After graduating, he began working for General Motors. For the last nine years, he has worked in the financial field and has become a senior Vice President of a major American financial institution.

Henry, together with his wife, Lada, and their two daughters, Ilene (left) and Regina (right).

We love our son and have always treated his interests and goals with respect. I have always been and will continue to be proud of him. Henry is a special person, a person with a strong spirit and personality. In extreme situations we found that he not only held to his life's goal, but knew how to accomplish it. What an amazing and pleasant discovery for a parent!

I have always paid a lot of attention to my son. We tried to give him a good upbringing and education. I think the times we spent together during my annual vacations were especially valuable. There were many opportunities to sit and talk with each other. In his childhood, Henry always had a lot of questions. I guess I was quite good at answering them. But even now I remember two questions I could not answer. As a child he once asked, "Where did the very first man come from?" As a teenager he asked the second question, "Why was not I born in America?"

Now Henry and his wife Lada have two beautiful, smart and inquisitive daughters, Ilene and Regina. On the one hand, it is more difficult for him to answer his children's questions that modern science might raise but can hardly answer. On the other hand, it is much easier for him, as he will never need to answer the second of the questions I found so difficult.

Hello, My Future

My granddaughters Ilene (13) and Regina (10) are our family's first generation born in the USA. They are great in scholastics, music and sports and are blessed with wonderful friends. According to the All-American *Tests of Basic Skills* Ilene has been recently recognized in the top 1% of sixth grade students nationally.

Chapter 16

WHAT IF?

I t was May 2004. Four people sat in our living room: my friends Victor and Max, my cousin Mara, and me, I.D., the nickname that my friends have called me since childhood.

Victor is an engineer and a creator of a new method for cold welding metal. He is a well-educated and cultured person. He was described as '"intellectual" even when we were twelve or thirteen years old.

Max worked for construction companies for forty-five years. We always considered him a frank, direct, and fair person. We loved him for his personality. However, we used to call him the "Plain Man." He believes there is always an easy, simple way to be honest and truthful, with nothing in between. Age has done little to change his nature, principles, and moral values.

We had not been together for several years, so we had a lot of things to remember and discuss. It was a special reunion, exactly fifty years since we had graduated together from the same high school in the Ukraine.

My cousin Mara was a guest of Victor's wife. She came to Canada and America from Australia for a couple of weeks. I was very happy to see her again. We have a close relationship and deep respect for each other. While this good-hearted woman is only six years older than I am, she has always treated me as a person of the younger generation. There is a reason for this.

When Mara was a girl of seven, she witnessed my natural mother Cecilia's suffering during her last days of life and remembered how she held my hands in hers. Any time when we are together she is reminded of this memory, and thus considered herself much older than I am. I know Mara and her protectiveness well. She will not tolerate any criticism of me and really is unable to be objective about anything concerning me.

We all were happy to see each other, extremely exited, and good-humoredly noted the changes in our appearances. We began to recall our school, former classmates, and the simple tricks we played. It is fascinating that we have kept these memories for more than a half a century. That evening we had a lot of fun, often forgetting about our age and family problems. But although reminiscing was wonderful, we eventually returned to real life.

In particular, my friends began to discuss some issues concerning my book and, even more, my life in general.

Some of my published books, articles, and official letters were on the table. Max selected three of them. One of them was a letter of recommendation written by the President of the USA-Russian Business Council in Washington, DC, who was extremely generous in his praise of me and my experiences. I have never before, or after, received such compliments. The next was an official letter in which I was asked to be a consulting advisor on a twenty-month UN Funded Project for the government of a Central Asian country.

Finally, there was a short article entitled "Ahead of His Time", about my academic and business experiences, published in Moscow four days before my emigration to the USA. It was Max who brought me two copies of this article when I was at Moscow's International Airport spending my last hour before leaving my home forever. It was written by P. Borschchevsky and published in *Business World* on December 8, 1992. I quote the main points of it here:

> *Doctor of Economics Izyaslav Darakhovskiy, who attached a great importance to market elements in national economy management, has always been far ahead of his colleagues when the "market" was a forbidden theme for discussion among economists. He wrote a total of 100 articles, brochures, and books, including "All About

Group of participants at the International Seminar in Paris.

Marketing," "Business and Manager," and "Marketing Service at your Enterprise."

*Izyaslav Darakhovskiy is one of the founders and scientific advisor to the Union of Entrepreneurs and Leaseholders.

*His participation in scientific meetings in Hungary, France, Germany and the USA have earned him considerable renown abroad.

Max declared, after looking at these three selected papers, that even this limited information about myself can convince an objective person that this was the life of a happy and fortunate person.

"I know," Max said, "that you experienced a broad spectrum of emotions: joy and grief, love and hatred, ups and downs, admiration and envy. From your life we can discover much about the 20th century, from bloody wars to the massive annihilation of your own people during peace time at the hands one of the most dangerous dictators throughout history, Joseph Stalin. You witnessed the hopeful dream and bleak reality of collective property and planned economy, and saw Gorbachev's careful reforms and painful attempts to revive the free economy for Eastern Europe and the other Asian Communist countries affected one-third of the world's population. You lived a military, industrial and academic life, mimicking the progress of civilization toward today's global politics and economies. Moving from the fear to assert your own views about simple social issues to courageously expressing candid observations about the collapse of one of the most powerful Empires of the 20th century."

"But most importantly," he indicated, "your's is a personal

story, the story of a man whose fate and difficult social circumstances have given him little rest for many decades. You survived and reached significant personal achievements. That is why your life experiences are interesting and inspiring."

Victor suggested softly that he knows me as well as Max and had some different views about my life. Victor always was good with details. After he made some mathematical calculations he concluded that I did not contribute to society in full measure for about fifteen years. For that period of time I could have worked in academia or business. Victor continued with this line of thought. I was two years late beginning school. It took five years before I was allowed to become a University student. At fifty-seven I was officially a resident of the United States. Yet, since then I had not been able to secure a full-time job as a scientist or businessman.

This was a seeming contradiction to the statements previously made by Max. According to one friend I had led a fulfilling and accomplished life but the other friend's views were drastically different. There is an unwritten rule amongst us that anyone can speak his opinion about the other two in ways that may surprise or shock outsiders. We have known each other for a long time and our friendship has been tested by time, distance, and significant difference in life style. Our friendship began when we were children and our relationship has changed little over the years. However, I was still shocked by Victor's interpretation of my life, though I kept silent.

Max, however, was unable to control himself. He stated that nobody could possibly share Victor's opinion. How could anyone consider years spent in military service or working hard in agriculture a waste of time? Max really did not understand his friend's way of thinking. He proclaimed that Victor's mathematical calculations had nothing to do with reality.

To Max, I had started school late for such a "trifling" reason: the Nazis did not open or build schools for children in ghettos and camps. Because of "special care" from another despot, Soviet ruler Joseph Stalin, thousands of young people with good knowledge and capabilities tried for years to get a college education and a profession, but were not able to overcome the social barriers faced by people of my nationality.

Finally, Max said, "He came to a new country at the age of 57. He did not speak English and was not yet an American citizen. Even people born in America have great difficulty starting a new career at that age. It took a couple of years to adapt to the new circumstances and overcome cultural and language barriers until you began to make progress. He lectured and published articles in English and was involved in different projects for American companies, including the some of the most prestigious financial institutions. He even did volunteer work. I can't accept Victor's 'verdict' on Izyaslav Darahovskiy's life as 'unproductive.'"

I listened to my friends' debate very carefully, but I also watched Mara. I knew without doubt that she would defend me. But when she began to speak, I was amused by the way she chose to get to the point. Instead of emphasizing only what I had done, she spoke of how easily things might have gone differenly. Her key words were, "What if ?"

Mara told my friends that I am a successful man, and that she was going to prove it point by point. She surprised us all by using phrases and words that were not normally part of her vocabulary. I knew that her life had never been an easy one. She married at a young age and was soon divorced. She endured many family difficulties, never had the opportunity to get a good education, and worked for fifty years as a barber. We were all very attentive to her speech.

"He is publishing his book, a story about a life with very broad and varied experiences, a story about lifestyles in other parts of the world." I tried to gently remind her that I still had doubts that this book would be published soon. She ignored me, continuing, "He wrote a book in a language that, ten years ago, he did not speak. This will be his eighth book and the first in English. Isn't that success?"

"How many talented graduates tried to work for the Academy of Sciences in the former USSR? He was invited to work for this prestigious institution when he was an undergraduate student. It happened because of his knowledge, capability, and high aspirations. But there are always more talented and gifted people than openings. So he also had prospects of getting a job at a factory as an economist with modest financial benefits and satisfaction. Wouldn't you agree that this man was born under a lucky star?"

"It is difficult to comprehend the social, national, and other kinds of barriers people of our nationality had to overcome to get a Ph.D., and especially the second Doctorate Degree. I.D. was told plainly that usually only one of dozens of minority aspirants came up a winner. He won, even though he had little chance of success. If this had not happened, his life might have been much less interesting and creative than it became. Isn't he a lucky person?"

She continued about many other events of my life. What if I hadn't gone to college, hadn't been rescued after a gang beating during my vacation in Georgia on the Black Sea, had died during 1000 days in the Nazi concentration camp or during the two years of the great famine in the Ukraine after the WWII?

Continuing, she took me all the way back to the first days and months of my life. What if as a newborn boy I had become infected with blood poisoning, like my mother, and. . .

My friends and I, as we had often done in the past, reacted simultaneously: "There wouldn't be a person named I.D. at all, and today's discussion would not have happened!"

We all laughed, even Mara. But my cousin's unusual logic had provided an interesting and stimulating perspective on the past nearly seventy years of my life. After all she had said, how could I not consider myself extremely fortunate?

The four of us became relaxed, feeling as carefree as we had been in our youth. Victor made the final point. Everyone expressed an opinion about me, he said, but why had I kept silent? In response, I quoted this phrase:

So many roads have been traveled,

So many mistakes have been made.

I had always tried, I told them, to be the master of my own life. Which had been greater: unique experiences or everyday life, happiness or sadness? Did my life involve only theoretical knowledge, or was it practical and useful? Was it merely difficult, or interesting and even inspiring?

Let the reader be the judge.